PADDLERS' GUIDE
for
TREATING
MEDICAL
EMERGENCIES

OCT   '06

PADDLERS' GUIDE
for
TREATING
MEDICAL
EMERGENCIES

Patrick Brighton, M.D., F.A.C.S.

MENASHA RIDGE PRESS
BIRMINGHAM, ALABAMA

Library of Congress Cataloging-in-Publication Data

Brighton, Patrick, 1962–
    Paddlers' guide for treating medical emergencies / Patrick
Brighton.—1st ed.
        p. cm.
    ISBN 0-89732-629-6
    1. First aid in illness and injury. 2. Canoeing accidents. 3. Canoes
and canoeing—Safety measures. 4. Medical emergencies. I. Title.

RC88.9.B6B75 2005
616.02'5—dc22

                                                    2005049628

Illustrations by Tami Knight
Text design by Clare Minges
Cover design by Travis Bryant

Menasha Ridge Press
P.O. Box 43673
Birmingham, AL 35243
www.menasharidge.com

TABLE *of* CONTENTS

ACKNOWLEDGMENTS

Don't you love it when the Academy Award winners launch into a 30-minute speech in which they thank everyone from the person who cuts the hair around their poodle's butt to Aunt Martha's financial adviser?

There are, however, a number of people who made this work possible, so if you enjoy any portion of it, send your thanks to them. Firstly, Bob Sehlinger at Menasha Ridge Press, who called me out of the blue and said, "Why don't you get off your *tokhes* and do something constructive?" That's paraphrased, by the way. Also, Russell Helms, Molly Merkle, and the rest of the wonderful Menasha Ridge staff. Next, Tami Knight, who has been kind enough to share with us her unsurpassed wit and insight through her illustrations.

Finally, I would like to say thank you to the person who has been my constant companion for the last ten years, and who has truly shown me what it means to be able to enjoy a peaceful, balanced life—my dear wife, Kimberley.

PADDLERS' GUIDE
for
TREATING
MEDICAL
EMERGENCIES

INTRODUCTION

When I first set pen to paper (OK, finger to keyboard) for this book, I thought: "How the heck can I write an entire book on medical care for paddlers?" Then I realized that paddling encompasses an incredible range of activities from serenely drifting through the boundary waters of the north-central United States, to kayaking the Tsangpo Gorge in southeastern Tibet, and everything in between. Then I thought, "Paddlers can really get into some deep doo-doo. How the heck can the medical care for all these varied activities be covered in *only* one book?"

Another interesting fact about medical emergencies while paddling is that when bad things happen, they can happen instantaneously. If those bad things occur, and you are underwater at the time and don't happen to be a trout, it can make for a really bad day.

Jesting aside, all paddling nourishes the emotionally starved soul, stimulates the fluorescent-light-poisoned mind and body, and is also a shitload of fun. But please always remember—water can turn deadly in an instant. There are too many water-related deaths every year—most could have been prevented (yeah, I know, sit in the Lazy Boy, drink cheap beer, watch the professional sport de jour, and you'll never drown paddling). It doesn't matter if you are floating peacefully across Jenny Lake or rodeoing Class-IV water in the Ocoee—if strange things happen and you find yourself trapped on the lesser-oxygenated side of the surface, you will die—in four minutes or less. So please be thoughtful in regard to paddling decisions. Also, if you do find yourself in the position of needing to administer aid to a person who has nearly drowned or sustained a serious injury, as difficult as it might be, you must remain calm (yeah, right). I understand that this flies in the face of every emotion and thought that arises, especially when it is a loved one who is in a life-threatening crisis, but this is the only way that a positive outcome can be achieved.

There may come a time when extremely quick thought and action are required, but remember, no one dies in two seconds: you always have time to think—even if just for a few seconds (cognitive thought is what separates bipeds from butternut squash). If someone were to sustain an injury that claimed his life within two seconds, there would certainly have been nothing you could have done anyway.

So, read this manual before you set out on your water adventure, process what you would do in several medical emergency scenarios, and for God's sake, get out and get wet.

(MEDICATIONS)

Dispensing

Medications—chemicals synthesized from raw materials ruthlessly extracted from our rapidly vanishing rain forests only to enhance our already pathetically easy existence… wait a minute, wrong speech. Anyway, medications really are beneficial—even essential in certain emergencies outdoors. Most medications are administered orally (*per os,* for you Latin speakers). However, certain medications can be administered only by injection, either into a muscle or vein, and still others are given via inhalation, through patches applied to the skin, or by insertion into the rectum (wait a minute, I don't think I know you that well…). Most medications— ibuprofen, Claritin, and so on—are given orally and we are all familiar with taking medications this way. In a medical emergency, however, the victim may not be conscious, may have an obstructed airway, or may not be able to otherwise swallow medications. Do not ever attempt to give a victim medications by mouth under these circumstances, or if you have any concern that a pill may end up in his airway instead of his stomach.

ORAL   As discussed above, you may give medications to a person who is awake and cooperative and has a clear airway. Remember that medications given by mouth require at least 30 minutes to take effect, so you would probably not give medications this way in a true emergency.

INJECTIONS   This is the most expeditious method of delivering immediately available medications, but injections should be administered only by trained personnel. Improperly administering parenteral (injectable) medications can be much more lethal than not giving any medication. There are only a handful of injectable medications that one might potentially use, and these would typically be administered only in dire emergencies by trained rescue personnel.

INHALANTS   Inhaled medications are usually those that a person takes routinely: asthma or allergy meds, for instance. Administering assistance with these medications usually involves helping a person find her steroid asthma inhaler.

PATCHES   There is little reason to administer medications by patch in a medical emergency. The medication absorbs slowly and predictably, usually over 6 to 24 hours—too much time to be of much use in the short term.

SUPPOSITORIES   This is actually an excellent way to administer some medications and to break the ice in certain hard-to-start relation-ships. As weird as it sounds, medications dissolve and are absorbed in the inside lining (mucosa) of the rectum quite efficiently. This is a handy way to get some drugs circulating in victims who are nause-ated or are otherwise unable to take medications by mouth. Antinau-sea medications and Tylenol are the most commonly administered rectal medications. Regarding technique, you must make sure (1) that the medication and the (one hopes) gloved finger that is placing the suppository are well lubricated (with KY jelly, olive oil, water, etc.); and (2) that the medication is positioned at least one to two inches inside the rectum. This will ensure that the medicine is within the confines of the rectum, where it can be absorbed.

Precautions

Here comes the cautionary advice. Please, please, please only carry medications that you personally are familiar with administering; you must completely understand their dosage as well as their possible side effects and potential interactions with other medications.

Disclaimer

And now for the legal portion of our program: All medications—that's right *all*—including Tylenol, ibuprofen, and even oxygen, can be lethal if administered inappropriately. The advice in this text represents what I would anticipate doing, having studied medicine and trained in this field for 20-odd years. As with most things in life, there are usually several ways to achieve a positive result in an emergency, so I recommend gathering as much information as you can—beginning with this book—and applying that information in a thoughtful manner compatible with the situation.

...[1]...

EYES, EARS, AND NOSE

EYES

Wonderful organs, the eyes, but we don't actually pay much attention to them unless we happen to stick a river knife into one.

Foreign Body in the Eye

PREVENTION TIP
Don't stick anything in your eye.

MORE USEFUL PREVENTION TIP
The eye has a wonderful protection device—the eyelid. This protects the eye from most objects traveling toward it. The kicker is that you have to see the object coming. It follows that the objects most commonly contacting the eyeball are things that you don't see coming, such as eyelashes, windblown small objects, or cinders from a campfire. Therefore, during higher-danger times, such as on windy days, when bushwhacking through brush, at night, and especially around a fire, or when wending your way through thick Florida mangrove swamps in a dugout canoe, consider protective eyewear—wraparound glasses, for example.

TREATMENT

Do not stick your finger or anything else in your eye (or rub your eyelid) to attempt to dislodge the object already in your eye. Really, this is a bad idea. Your grandmother told you the same thing, and look how good her eyes were (OK, bad example). However, you do risk converting an easily treatable situation into a protracted nightmare that may jeopardize your vision, such as a deep corneal laceration or a raging eye infection.

Do wash your eye copiously with water. A hydration bladder with a slit-type mouthpiece (such as a CamelBak, Platypus, etc.) works beautifully. Please make sure there is clean water, not beer, in the bladder. If it still feels like there is something there (I say "feel" because the object may be gone, but an abrasion or laceration may make it feel like there's a tree in there), you may have a companion try to look (no touching!), so that he can direct the irrigation appropriately.

If you have tried this until you are thoroughly waterlogged, but it still feels like something is in there, and no one can see it, cover the eye with a bandage (using tape or head wrap over the bandage or eye patch), and head to an ophthalmologist or the ER immediately. Yes, it really is that important.

Retinal Burn

The retina is a sensory membrane in the very back of the eye that receives incoming light, allowing you to see the upcoming Class-VI rapids that you are about to go through—sideways. It is also very sensitive to bright lights and, like the skin, can become sunburned. Besides being very painful, this can lead to temporary or even permanent vision loss.

PREVENTION TIP

Make sure the only pad-
dling you do is in a
heated wading pool at
the South Pole in the
dead darkness of the aus-
tral winter.

**MORE USEFUL
PREVENTION TIP**

Just like sex with
strangers: "protection,
protection, protection."
Retinas begin to suffer
damage almost immedi-
ately upon direct expo-
sure to ultraviolet (UV)
rays, so put on protective
eyewear with complete
UVA and UVB block (this

will be clearly stated on good-quality sunglasses) *before* you set out.

If your plan is to combat roll down the upper Gauley, UV protective eyewear may not be as important as it would be if you were to
float placidly amid the feeding humpback whales in Glacier Bay on a
bright July day. Remember, sunlight reflects wonderfully off water to
penetrate under and around eyewear that does not closely conform to
your face. Glaciers and snowfields make an even better reflector.

TREATMENT

The retina demonstrates similar (but not identical) healing patterns as
the skin when burned. Like skin, unless the innermost lining of the
retina is burned (highly unusual), the retina will regenerate. This will
take time, however. Unlike skin, we cannot put salves or ointments on
the retina to protect it and speed healing. What we do instead is cover
the eyes to prevent more incoming light (and possibly more damage to
injured retinas) and allow the retinal cells some down time for regen-
eration to occur. This is a roundabout way of saying: put patches on
both eyes to completely occlude incoming light, then see a good ophthalmologist (retinal specialist) immediately.

How do you know if you have a retinal burn? It ain't subtle (just like getting gonorrhea after unprotected sex—you know what you did wrong). After exposure, your eyes will burn and hurt terribly, particularly when open. This usually happens within minutes but can worsen over the course of 12 hours or more. The symptoms will persist after the sun goes down.

As with sunburns, there are varying degrees of bad here. Retinal burns range from mildly painful with essentially no impact on vision to terribly painful with temporary or permanent blindness.

EARS

Ears—I love 'em. Just think—if you didn't have ears, your ultra-chic UV-protection sunglasses would slide right off your head (unless your nose is like Klinger's on *M*A*S*H*). Around 99.9% of the time they are maintenance-free appendages. Let's chat about the other 0.1%, shall we?

Foreign Body in the Ear

Despite what the term implies, a foreign body does not represent a deceased Mongolian but rather a weird, unnatural object lodged (usually painfully) in the ear canal. The aforementioned object has almost always (99.9% of the time) been placed in that location by the owner of said ear canal. This factoid segues nicely into our next topic: Prevention Tip.

PREVENTION TIP
With a commercial, pneumatic staple gun, staple your hands to your upper thighs.

MORE USEFUL PREVENTION TIP
One of the very first things I learned in medical school (right after "never eat spaghetti in the operating room") was from a sage and learned professor who said, "Never stick anything smaller than your elbow in your ear." Hmmmmmmm...

Similar to the eye, the ear is a very complicated and sensitive organ—no, not the protrusions you hang your glasses on, but the inner workings. Even though you may use a Q-tip at home when your ear itches (despite medical advice to the contrary) and get away with it, try the same maneuver with an old straightened-out grommet scavenged from your river raft and things may turn out differently. You definitely risk a laceration (cut) to the external ear canal, which often becomes infected, or a puncture of the eardrum, which often leads to at least partial hearing loss.

TREATMENT

Gently washing the ear out (lavage) is the only reasonable way to dislodge a foreign body from an ear. It would be rare for someone to have a bulb syringe—a soft lightbulb-shaped thing that ENT (ear, nose, and throat) docs use—but if one is available, you may have a companion gently lavage the ear with warm water. I have not tried this, but the water bladder from your hydration system may also work well. You can have someone squeeze the bladder to deliver more pressure. (*Note:* If water enters one ear and exits the other, stop, take a digital picture, and e-mail it to me immediately.) Do make sure the water is warm, not hot or cold, and *do not* stick the syringe, water bladder, or anything else into the ear canal. If this does not work, you will have to see an ENT specialist or go to the ER. This is not an absolute emergency—if it does not hurt too much or drive you too bonkers. Obviously, earlier care is better.

Things change somewhat if a live critter takes up residence in your external ear canal. I did once have a spider crawl into my ear and perform all the acts of *River Dance* on my eardrum. Needless to say, I spent a few interesting hours until my ENT friend could wash out the offending arachnid. All kidding aside—a live insect moving against your eardrum is really uncomfortable. You may try a few drops of warm (not hot!) olive oil in your ear while lying with your uninhabited ear toward the ground. This works a surprising percentage of the

time. If this fails, you can try the lavage method. If this still fails to dislodge the squatter, you guessed it—it's ER time.

NOSE

How important is the human nose? There are so many answers to this question: absolutely critical for warming and humidifying dry, cold air prior to inspiration; indispensable for filtering airborne particles so that the lungs remain clear for efficient gas exchange; and so on and so forth.

Nosebleeds

We've all experienced the wonderful sensation of a nosebleed a few times—the warm red gush down our chins during a particularly sensitive social event, the dark crusty boogers we get to pick afterward, and so on. Given the fact that essentially all 7 billion humans on the planet have experienced this phenomenon, there must be an explanation—right? Excellent observation! OK, here it is: Because the primary function of the nose is to warm and humidify incoming air, a huge plexus of blood vessels lives just below the surface of the very thin inside lining of the nose. These blood vessels function as both heat exchanger and humidifier. Pretty cool, huh? Therefore, our tip to prevent nosebleeds is as follows: find a friend with small, soft hands—a small manicurist, for instance—and then, when you feel a small crusty deep in the ol' schnoz, grab one of your friend's small fingers to fish it out.

PREVENTION TIP
Don't pick your nose with a steam shovel.

MORE USEFUL PREVENTION TIP
Besides using your nose as a battering ram against some unyielding object, the most common cause of nosebleeds is drying of the inside lining of the nose (the mucosa). One of the primary functions of the nose is to humidify incoming air so that really dry air does not rush in and damage fragile lungs. This mucosal drying out obviously happens more in climates where the humidity of the outside air is much less than that inside your nose—that is, in the southwestern United States, on the Tibetan Plateau, in Antarctica, and so on. If you know you are prone to nosebleeds, you may want to take along a saline nasal spray.

TREATMENT
You can stop almost all nosebleeds by using the treatment your grandmother told you about (man, was she smart):

(1) Lean against something with your head tilted back a little bit—some people recommend that you lie down, but then the blood runs down the back of your throat and makes you gag—yuck!

(2) Squeeze firmly with your fingers (or better yet, your buddy's) on both sides of the nose where the fleshy part meets the hard part. There is no sense in squeezing the hard part, as this is bone and will have no effect on stemming the red tide. It may take five to ten minutes, or even longer, for the bleeding to stop. In the unusual situation in which this doesn't work after a reasonable period of time (30 to 45 minutes), or if blood continues to pour down the back of the person's throat while pressure is being held, a more difficult problem may exist. This likely indicates a posterior nosebleed. No, not *that* posterior. If this appears to be the case, have someone in the party get medical help immediately. If medical help will not be available for several hours, you will have to try something else

Tampon nasal-packing technique

to stop the bleeding. This involves packing the nose. Again, do not attempt this unless experienced medical help is not readily forthcoming, as there is some risk of internal damage. Nasal packing is very uncomfortable for the victim, but if this becomes necessary, here is how to do it.

By far the best material for nasal packing is a tampon. Tampons are usually close to the right size, they have a string for extraction, and they expand when wet to apply auto-pressure. Nasal-packing tampons are available but are hard to find. Take a tampon out of its applicator, and sensitively, but with some firmness, insert one into each nostril. If you aim it correctly (more *in* than *up*), it is surprising how far it will go. Stop if you hit something solid or if the person complains of a sudden severe increase in pain. If tampons are not available, then gauze, a clean handkerchief, or such may be substituted. I have actually used the tampon technique numerous times, and it usually works. If this succeeds in stopping the bleeding, do not remove the packing. Let medical personnel do this—the bleeding may recur, and you may not be as lucky next time.

NASAL TRAUMA

Nasal trauma, while unfortunately quite common, is also relatively insignificant (usually) in the grand scheme of things. A truism in life is that it is impossible to look at something without your nose pointing in that same direction. Furthermore, the fact that the nose is the most protuberant thing on your face means that if something is gonna get smacked, well, you can figure the rest out.

PREVENTION TIP
Do not call Mike Tyson a "girlie man."

MORE USEFUL PREVENTION TIP
I dunno, sit on the couch and lip synch old Elvis flicks.

TREATMENT
Nasal trauma typically involves a broken nose. Besides being very painful and causing some tearing from the eyes and enough bruising to make your face resemble one of Aunt Sophie's prizewinning eggplants, this is not typically a life-threatening emergency. If the nose does bleed excessively, treat as in "Nosebleeds" (page 10). If there are any associated lacerations, clean and cover them as you would any laceration (chapter 6) and seek medical care as soon as possible.

...[2]...

GASTROINTESTINAL DISORDERS

All of us have experienced various types of gastrointestinal (GI) upset, ranging from heartburn to nausea, vomiting, diarrhea, and constipation. The causes of these disorders number in the hundreds. We will cover a few of the common situations faced by paddlers, particularly those on extended river trips in the remote backcountry.

HEARTBURN

Also called acid-reflux disease, heartburn occurs when very acidic liquid, normally confined to the stomach, washes up into the esophagus—painful. If you have never experienced this phenomenon but wish to do so, you may try swallowing a burning charcoal briquette (not recommended). There are two basic scenarios: frequent heartburn (pathologic) and occasional heartburn. If you fall into the former category, you may already have a regimen of medications to help you through these bouts (you should also consult a GI specialist, if you haven't already done so). The occasional bout of heartburn covers most of the rest of us.

What typically happens on an extended river trip is that we paddle merrily for hours, stopping way too infrequently to refuel with snacks, sports drinks, and so on. Then we set up camp, eat a huge meal—because by then we are so hungry that we are digesting our

own spleens—immediately lie down in our sleeping bags, and then stay up half the night with napalm shooting up our throats. This occurs because our blood has been shunted to the big muscles of our legs during the day. So, after receiving the hastily chewed delight, our GI tracts are deprived of adequate blood to work properly. This results in the three quarts of beef 'n' mac sitting in our stomachs, and then rolling back up our throats when we lie down.

PREVENTION TIP
Try eating just two quarts of beef 'n' mac.

MORE USEFUL PREVENTION TIP
As hard as it may be, try to eat frequently (constantly, in my case) as you paddle—this will supply more calories during the day so that you don't have to pig out at night. By the way, if you keep your blood

sugar at a relatively constant level all day, you won't feel as fatigued and will be able to paddle farther and faster.

Try to eat your evening meal early, and don't stuff yourself! I would also avoid overly seasoned or spicy foods, and obviously those foods that you know you have trouble digesting. After dinner it is a good idea to get a little exercise—finish setting up camp, go for a short hike, try to separate yourself from your crusty underwear. That will give your food a chance to move through your digestive system a little.

TREATMENT

Really, the only effective treatment once heartburn has set in is to take one of the many medications available for this condition. This implies that you have brought some of these medications with you in your first-aid kit. General categories of these medications include:

(1) Antacids (Rolaids, Maalox, etc.). These are the first medications to use. They work essentially instantly, have few (if any) side effects, and are cheap.

(2) H2 blockers (Tagamet, Zantac). These work well and last longer than antacids but take longer to work and are more expensive.

(3) PPIs (Prilosec, Nexium, Prevacid). These are the most efficient at neutralizing stomach acid and last much longer (up to 24 hours) but take longer to start working than do H2 blockers and are the most expensive. If you are particularly reflux-prone, you may want to take antacids plus an H2 blocker or PPI.

NAUSEA, VOMITING, AND DIARRHEA

All of us have experienced the GI tract's (our gut's) contents spewing forth from the north pole, the south pole, or both. The common theme here is that the cause relates typically to something we have put into our mouths—contaminated food, infected water, dirty hands, a partner's wet hiking sock, and such. To delve even further, the tiny culprits we ingest that cause our GI distress are bacteria, viruses, single-cell or small organisms, and toxins (usually from bacteria).

PREVENTION TIP

Refuse to shake hands with strangers and decline invitations to share straws.

MORE USEFUL PREVENTION TIP

Clearly, if the organisms that make us ill live in contaminated material that we put into our mouths, then all we have to do is not put that contaminated material into our mouths in the first place (yes, I finished all four years of medical school). Aha! Preparing to avoid potential sources of contamination requires forethought and planning.

Water

Most freshwater sources (probably greater than 90% of them) in areas where people travel, even in the remote backcountry, are contaminated—primarily by giardia and/or cryptosporidium. Several different types of pathologic (disease-causing) viruses are also found in most water sources. While I have several friends who routinely do not treat their drinking water (mainly guides with extensive backcountry experience, I strongly encourage (very strongly recommend) that everyone treat all drinking water in some way.

Ways to treat drinking water

METHOD	PRO	CON
Boiling (to at least 160° for five minutes)	• Don't have to carry iodine or water purifier • Very effective	• Impractical on the trail • Uses fuel • Difficult at higher elevations (because water boils at lower temperatures, boiling may not be as effective)
Filters	• Work very well • Water tastes good	• Heavy • Clog often and must be washed • May not work at all in very dirty water, despite what manufacturers say
Chemical Tablets, Liquids	• Lightweight • Very effective	• Can affect taste • Iodine turns water and containers brown • Takes 15–30 minutes to work; even longer with cold water

My wife and I use a bromine-based liquid (Aqua Mira) that comes in two bottles. You mix them together, wait five minutes, then dump them into your full water containers. We have not had any problems over the years with this system.

Food

Just as at home, food—especially meat—must be cooked properly (thoroughly enough to kill harmful microorganisms). Remember that at higher altitudes water boils at a lower temperature than the 212°F required at sea level, (200°F at 6,500 feet; 194°F at 10,000 feet, and so on). So, unless you enjoy hauling umpteen gallons of stove fuel with you, try bringing precooked foods that you can reheat or rehydrate.

Fecal-Oral Contamination (FOC)

Fecal-oral contamination. Ugghhh! I always shudder when I see those words. However, we must discuss them because this is the most frequent means of introducing pathologic GI organisms into the body.

By no means should one infer that in order to get sick, one must dine on a plate of freshly produced poop. But that is, to some degree, what happens. As gross as it sounds, when we defecate in the great outdoors where our cleanliness may be questionable (OK, I'll speak for myself), we frequently collect some bacteria on our hands when we wipe. Then, if we don't wash up properly afterward—often overlooked in the absence of hot and cold running water and watermelon-scented soap—these bacteria transfer to our food because we typically eat and wipe with the same hand. It may seem excessive to spell this situation out in such graphic detail, but this is probably the most frequent and readily preventable malady that can absolutely ruin a paddling trip.

PREVENTION TIP

Build up your tolerance to fecal bacteria by engaging in reciprocal grooming sessions with your golden retriever.

MORE USEFUL PREVENTION TIP

So, how do you prevent FOC? Simple. Wash your hands with at least water—soap is preferable—*immediately* after you poop. Do not pet the dog, make oatmeal for your paddling friends, or do anything else. Wash your hands every time, and then—this is really important—use that waterless, disappearing disinfectant (Purell or another brand).

This stuff really works; hospitals are now putting dispensers outside every patient's room and in all the nursing stations. It is also resistant to freezing, even at temperatures well below 32°F. Studies have shown that consistent use of this goop has decreased hospital-acquired infections by more than 90%.

TREATMENT

OK, now you're sick, lying in your tent on the bank of the Orinoco River in southern Venezuela, having just paddled 2,000 miles in a dugout canoe, spewing forth vile substances from top and bottom. There are two objectives here:

(1) Take care of the ill effects already produced by the offending invaders.

(2) Kill the organisms off and prevent further damage.

To accomplish the first objective, you and your friends (I'm making an assumption here) have to make sure that you don't become dehydrated and throw your electrolytes (sodium, potassium) out of whack. It would also be nice to alleviate your symptoms of nausea and vomiting.

Fluids are essential—especially electrolyte solutions, such as Gatorade, Cytomax, and Gookinaid. Even if you throw up most of what you drink, it is essential to keep pounding the drinks. Antiemetic tablets or suppositories reduce nausea and vomiting (Phenergan works very well but requires a prescription and makes you drowsy). For diarrhea, Lomotil or Imodium work the best.

Unless you packed a laboratory with a scanning electron microscope, you don't know whether the illness is a result of bacteria, viruses, or what. It is reasonable to try a course of short-term oral antibiotics—taking 500 mg of Ciprofloxacin every 12 hours for two or three days frequently works well. A word here—there is some controversy (as with every topic in medicine, it seems) as to whether an empiric course of antibiotics should be used. Loosely translated, empiric means "I have no idea in hell what the problem is, but I'd better try something so I don't look like an idiot." In my opinion, however, this is typically a safer course than letting a potentially treatable infection go unchecked in the wilderness. Cipro, Levaquin, or a similar antibiotic has a low incidence of side effects, and the range of bacteria they kill is very large. Ask your physician for more information. As with every recommendation in this book, this only represents what I would do. You must make up your own mind, but this is a very common solution among experienced backcountry paddlers.

Most GI infections will subside in 12 to 24 hours, but if the symptoms persist or worsen, then evacuation should be considered.

...[3]...

CPR

This is the chapter that I hope everyone will read for a general knowledge base (and high-quality entertainment) but will never have to use. Before we delve into this chapter, please understand that this is a rudimentary treatment of a very complex topic. I highly encourage everyone to attend a wilderness medicine course where CPR (cardiopulmonary resuscitation) is taught, or at the very least to become CPR certified through a local hospital, the Red Cross or other certifying agency. In this guide we will discuss the use of CPR in situations in which a person has suffered an injury or illness so severe that it makes them unable to maintain their own breathing or heartbeat. Being dead obviously represents the most extreme stress a victim can experience and is no picnic for his friends, companions, and/or rescuers.

I have performed or helped with CPR perhaps a hundred times, and I have cried after almost all of those—and that is with people I don't know. Imagine a situation in which a family member or close friend is the patient, deep in a river gorge far from professional medical help. Talk about the ultimate shit-your-pants moment. This is the time where you as a rescuer absolutely must detach yourself as an emotionally involved friend and perform in a logical, expeditious (but not frenzied) manner. Difficult? Yes, but no other option exists if your companion is to survive.

The reasons that a person's heart may stop and/or breathing cease are far too numerous and involved to cover here. But the basics of how to deal with the situation, regardless of cause, are the same. It's similar to paddling on an unfamiliar lake or bay—you may not know the path, but if you are a competent navigator, you possess the skills to find your way.

Some of the most frequent backcountry emergency situations are caused by:

(1) Heart attack (myocardial infarction, MI)

(2) Lightning strike

(3) Choking

(4) Major trauma

We will outline the basics that apply to all situations and then detail a few specifics for the above conditions.

First, if you know or suspect that someone has stopped breathing, you must ascertain that this is indeed the case. At normal temperatures a person has approximately four minutes after breathing stops before irreversible brain damage occurs (30 seconds in my case). This means that you have some time to really make sure that your buddy has not just lain down for a peaceful moment of silent meditation before you start forcing your beef jerky–laced, haven't-brushed-in-three-days breath down his throat. Obviously, you will have some indication that something is terribly wrong: a lightning strike or long fall has occurred. If such an event occurred and the person does not appear to be breathing on his own, take a deep breath and think "A-B-C." You will read this many times in this chapter, and even after 20 years in the business, I still repeat this to myself at the start of an emergency.

A—Airway: Make sure he doesn't have a piece of teriyaki chicken, his tongue, a cow turd, or something else blocking the trachea (windpipe).

B—Breathing: Ensure that breathing has indeed stopped. Expose his chest and watch for the chest to rise and fall. You can also put your ear directly on either side of the chest and listen for sounds of breathing.

1) Check airway for blockage.

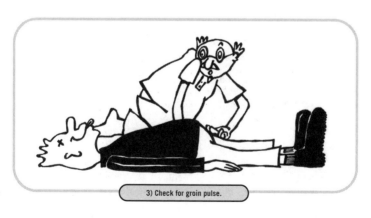

2) Check for chest rise and fall, and listen for breathing.

3) Check for groin pulse.

C—Circulation: Assess whether or not the heart is pumping blood. Many people suggest feeling the neck for a carotid pulse. I have always had a

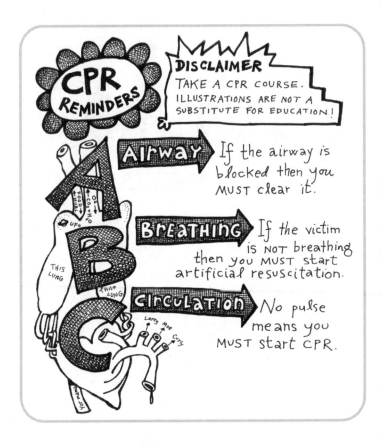

hard time with this, especially on muscular or chunky people. I have had better luck feeling the pulse right at the bend of the hip in the groin between the pubic bone and the hip bone.

Why are the A-B-Cs so important? It is imperative that you as a rescuer know whether the person has stopped breathing only, or if the heart has stopped as well. You don't want to start chest compressions on someone who has a heartbeat. You can mess up the heart rhythm that he has, and you can break his ribs or sternum.

Once you have established that the person has stopped breathing and that there is no obvious obstruction in the airway (check visually, and finger sweep the mouth if you have any doubts), then

CHILD VICTIM; (< 80 lbs)
one rescuer
- Support head tilted back *do NOT do this if you suspect neck injury
- Seal nose AND mouth
- check for pulse : ONLY do CPR if there is no pulse
- Five small compressions followed by two small breaths into nose & mouth REPEAT

ADULT VICTIM;
one rescuer
- pinch nostrils together
- lift chin & tilt head back- Do NOT do this if you suspect neck injuries
- seal mouth and deliver two breaths. Release after each breath.
- 15 compressions on breast bone

CHILD VICTIM;
two rescuers

First rescuer: performs rescue breathing

performs chest compressions.

ADULT VICTIM:
two rescuers

First rescuer: performs rescue breathing

performs chest compressions.

begin to breathe for him. First tilt the head back slightly (with the person lying on his back) so that his nose sticks up in the air in the sniffing position (I call it the "Prince Charles position"—that may explain why I've never been invited to Buckingham Palace). You must be careful if you have any reason to suspect a neck injury. Don't jerk the head around and, if people are available, have someone hold his head still by placing her hands on either side of his face. For an adult, pinch the nose closed and breathe into the victim's mouth moderately forcefully, so that you see his chest rise. Blowing about 15 times per minute (one breath every four seconds) is sufficient. For a child (age five and younger), put your mouth over the nose *and* mouth. Here you will have to breathe faster: 20 to 30 times per minute. Younger means faster breaths. Obviously, you must lessen the force you use for children. The tendency here is to breathe *too* fast. This results not only in poor ventilation for the victim but also in light-headedness for the rescuer.

Now here comes the tricky part. If the victim's heart has also stopped, then someone must do chest compressions to circulate the blood that is being oxygenated by the rescuer's breathing. Ideally there are two or more rescuers. In this case a rescuer who is not performing the artificial respirations will take a position on the opposite side of the victim from the breather, place one palm on the back of the other hand, lock elbows, place hands directly on the victim's sternum (breastbone), and compress. This is a total-body movement, not an arm movement. You will become fatigued after about ten strokes if you try to muscle this. I have seen plenty of 120-pound nurses perform chest compressions almost effortlessly for 45 minutes while a hulking muscle-bound counterpart had to quit after five minutes. Kneel on sleeping pads, backpacks, or whatever to protect your knees and use the height advantage to improve leverage.

Make sure to time your compressions so that you don't compress at the same time that the breather is delivering a breath. Right at 60 times per minute (once every second) is appropriate for adults. Children breathe faster than adults, and their hearts beat faster. Toddlers' hearts may thump at a hundred beats per minute, so increase the rate of compressions accordingly. Obviously, you have to decrease the compression force you use on children.

For larger children, compressing the chest with one palm is sufficient. For toddlers, using two or three fingers is sufficient. Adults may require a compression depth of one to three inches. It will feel a little bit like compressing a properly inflated soccer ball. This is really a lot of force, and it will be difficult to get yourself to push on a loved one that hard. You can check that your compressions are adequate by having someone feel for a pulse while you give compressions. You may feel ribs or even the sternum break. We don't want that to happen, but if it does, ignore it—it can be dealt with later. Remember that children require proportionately less force.

In the event that you are the only rescuer, you will have to be both the compressor and the breather. Start with the breathing first: give two or three breaths, then move over and give 15 compressions. Move back over and give 2 breaths, then 15 compressions. Repeat this 2-breaths-and-15-chest-compressions cycle continuously.

It goes without saying that, with more than two people in the party, someone should go for help immediately.

How long do you continue CPR? Very tough question. If the victim spontaneously resumes breathing and heartbeat returns (check every one to two minutes or so), then stop. It is very uncomfortable to have some goober beating on your chest or forcing fetid breath into you when you don't need it. In the unfortunate event that the victim does not recover quickly, when to stop is a judgment call. Survivability decreases the longer CPR is required. After about 15 minutes the chance of a person surviving is very small. Having said this, I would probably continue for 45 minutes to an hour. Before you decide to stop, check very carefully that the victim has neither spontaneous respirations nor a heartbeat. Get others to check as well, if possible. If the victim has either, continue.

The only exception to this rule is if a person is hypothermic (page 35). A person can be essentially frozen for quite some time and then make a complete recovery when resuscitated and warmed back to normal body temperature. There have been countless examples of people becoming severely hypothermic, showing no signs of life, and then making full recoveries after persistent (many hours of) CPR and rewarming. If it's possible that a victim may have a low core body temperature (page 40), continue resuscitation efforts until help arrives and the person can be rewarmed. As the saying goes, "A person is not dead until he is warm and dead." OK, doctors say weird things.

HEART ATTACK (MYOCARDIAL INFARCTION)

CPR was developed pretty much for the massive-heart-attack scenario. There is a classic constellation of symptoms: crushing chest pain radiating to the jaw and/or left arm, sweating, nausea, rapid respirations, and pallor (paleness). Obviously, not all—and sometimes none—of these may be present in someone with an evolving MI. However, assume that a heart attack has occurred if someone stops breathing for no apparent reason, even if they do not show any of the classic signs. One hopes that you would know if one of your companions had a heart condition.

PREVENTION TIP
Go to Houston and get an artificial heart.

MORE USEFUL PREVENTION TIP
Eat properly, exercise regularly, don't smoke, drink a glass of red wine per day, blah, blah, blah. The appropriate measures are in order. However, if you are reading this, you are already in the middle of

nowhere or are planning your imminent repositioning thereto. Having said that, if you know that you or someone in your party has heart disease, or is at increased risk for heart disease (they have family members with heart disease, have had heart problems, etc.), you can at least be somewhat prepared by ensuring that the person has appropriate medication on hand and that everyone has some chewable aspirin in their first-aid kits. Giving a person a chewable aspirin at the very first signs of a heart attack can markedly reduce the damage from a heart attack.

TREATMENT
If the victim has any nitroglycerin tablets, put one or two under his tongue, not down his throat. Perform CPR as needed and as described above.

LIGHTNING STRIKE

This situation clearly falls into the crap-your-pants category. Fortunately, I have never been struck by lightning—either directly or via ground strike (despite what my older brother says). I have, however, been with a group of friends when a bolt struck a tree and knocked several of them to the ground. I was terrified, as will be the nonelectrified members of your party, should you have the misfortune of being struck. Either a direct hit or a ground conduction (when lightning strikes the ground a distance from the victim but still electrocutes him by conducting the electricity through standing water, wet ground, metal, etc.) may cause a person's heart to stop beating. Despite what logical thought might suggest, both direct and indirect hits are potentially survivable.

PREVENTION TIP
Ditch the 20-foot steel walking staff.

MORE USEFUL PREVENTION TIP
Avoid areas prone to lightning, especially if you know that lightning events occur during a specific part of the day, or if you know that a storm is imminent. See "Lightning Injuries" on page 81 for more information on dealing with thunderbolts and lightning.

Allow a person to cough and hack as long as they are able.

TREATMENT

You must begin CPR promptly. Be especially cautious, though. Do a quick check to make sure the strike victim doesn't have any severe trauma—especially to the neck. If they do, you should still perform CPR, but have someone stabilize the head and neck to avoid potential spinal-cord injury.

CHOKING

This condition is almost always obvious unless you happen to come across someone who has choked and subsequently become unconscious. If someone is choking, let her cough and hack and try to get it out. Do not immediately walk up and whack her on the back. If she happens to be inhaling when you whack her, the object can become lodged further down her windpipe. Also if she is coughing, it means she is still getting air into her lungs.

PREVENTION TIP
Chew your !%@# food!

MORE USEFUL PREVENTION TIP
See Prevention Tip above.

TREATMENT
If she is unable to inhale any air to cough and sputter, she will start to turn blue and look really panicky. *Now* do something—quickly. You must very quickly—explosively even—increase the pressure in her abdomen to force air out of her lungs to, in turn, shoot the offending object out through her mouth.

For adults this is best accomplished by the Heimlich maneuver: stand behind the victim, clasp both hands firmly together just below the person's sternum (the upper part of the abdomen called the solar plexus), and forcefully jerk toward your own solar plexus. You must do this as hard and fast as you can: a person can survive only about four minutes without oxygen. Keep doing the Heimlich until the object becomes dislodged. There is no point in starting CPR, because the airway is blocked. In the event of unconsciousness, roll her onto her back and, with both hands locked together, straddle her legs and forcefully push down on the solar plexus area and somewhat toward her head. When you do get the object dislodged, don't let her eat it again.

Heimlich maneuver

32

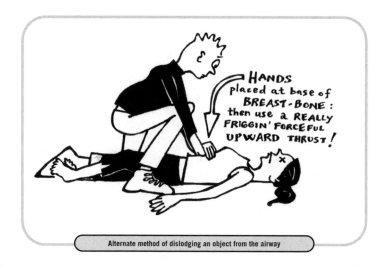

Alternate method of dislodging an object from the airway

For children small enough to pick up, you can grasp both their feet with one hand, lift them off the ground, and smack them sharply on the back (the child will be upside-down). If this does not work, lay them face up and push against the solar plexus with two or three fingers or however many is appropriate.

If you dislodge the object and the victim is still not breathing, then start CPR as described above.

MAJOR TRAUMA

In the very unfortunate and stressful situation in which someone in the party has suffered a major fall, been pelted by rockfall, or been so seriously injured that he is not breathing, has broken more than one bone, received lacerations, and suffered a head injury, you really just have to do the best you can.

PREVENTION TIP
Never paddle with someone who's given name is "Wildcat."

MORE USEFUL PREVENTION TIP
The best of plans go awry—and accidents do happen—but you can improve your odds if you treat all potentially dangerous situations like

a chess game; that is, set all your backup pieces in their optimal positions before you commit to the outing. In more concrete terms, this means taking all necessary emergency gear (first-aid kit, GPS, extra food, etc.), letting someone know of your specific plans before you set off, developing a backup plan or escape route, and so forth.

TREATMENT
Psychologically, it will be extremely difficult for you to get past the trauma injuries to figure out what to do. Again, breathe deeply and think "A-B-C." Stabilize the head and neck as best you can, clear the airway, and start breathing and performing compressions. The survival rate in this situation is exceedingly low, but try anyway.

...[4]...

EXTREME TEMPERATURE EXPOSURE
(HYPOTHERMIA AND HYPERTHERMIA)

Ask any ten-year-old what a normal *Homo sapien's* body temperature should be, and you will almost invariably hear, "I don't know; that's not on my Game Boy." Press them a little further and they will tell you "98.6° Fahrenheit." Since that answer is absolutely correct, and the number is so specific (not 98.5°F or 98.7°F), this tells us that humans operate within a very narrow temperature range. Granted, we can put on the latest synthetic blends when it gets cold, or seek shade when the sun blazes down on us, but when those external mechanisms fail, our ability to maintain ideal body temperature quickly deteriorates. Therefore, it becomes vital to recognize quickly when you or someone in your party overheats or overcools.

HYPOTHERMIA

Despite the fact that most of us only vaguely recognize that our skin does something more than separate our guts from the grimy sidewalk, our skin is an amazing organ (yes, the skin is a *bona fide* organ). For temperature regulation, the skin insulates our bodies (I'm guessing R-15), but its real genius lies in its ability to let heat out, or keep it in, depending on the ambient (outside) temperature. The skin accomplishes this amazing feat primarily by constricting or expanding the blood vessels in the skin; sweating is the other mechanism.

Sweating will be covered next, under hyperthermia. When the out-side air is significantly below 98.6°F, the vessels inside the skin con-strict, shunting the warm blood away from the skin to the vital internal organs, trying to keep the all-important core temperature at 98.6°F. Thus, when it is cold outside, your skin will feel cold, it will appear paler than normal, and those rope-like veins crisscrossing your ripped forearms will disappear. When this compensatory mecha-nism becomes overwhelmed, your core temperature begins to fall and you experience clinical hypothermia. It requires a dip of 2° to 3°F of core body temperature before you can get into serious trouble. As with any stressor, each person responds differently when hypothermic, but the general effects of progressive hypothermia are:

DEGREES FAHRENHEIT	HOW YOUR BODY RESPONDS
95–98.6	• Clear awareness of feeling cold
	• Moderate to severe shivering
	• Cold, pale skin
92–95	• Usually less aware of feeling cold
	• Wide range—severe to not much shivering
	• Skin is extremely cold, pale, almost corpse-like
88–92	• Almost never complains of cold; less lucid
	• Slow to react, or comatose
	• Usually not shivering
	• Skin as described above
< 88	• Lethal for most people—comatose
	• No shivering
	• Skin may actually feel warm as the skin blood vessels open; usually immediately preceding death

PREVENTION TIP

Move to Panama and never leave.

MORE USEFUL PREVENTION TIP

Two words: preparation and dryness. There are actually more than two words in the English language, but these are the two pertinent to this discussion. Anyway, given the incredible array of lightweight, warm, wicking clothing available, almost the only excuse to become hypothermic is to not have brought along enough of the appropriate clothing. Bring clothing for the worst possible conditions that you would historically encounter in your proposed area of travel.

The second vital step in warding off hypothermia is staying dry. Humans absolutely cannot maintain their body temperature if they are wet and the outside air is less than 98.6°F (unlikely on the banks of the Tellico in mid-January). It becomes critical therefore to maintain core body dryness (think Dry-Suit) when paddling in extremely cold environs.

TREATMENT

To repeat, if someone has become extremely hypothermic to the point that spontaneous breathing or heartbeat ceases, start CPR and continue CPR while someone else warms him *until his body temperature normalizes* (by which time one hopes you are in a hospital).

To warm a hypothermic victim in the field usually requires drying him first. Most clinically significant cases of hypothermia involve a person's becoming wet when the air temperature is only moderately

low (40° to 60°F) and
staying that way for at
least several hours.
However, the summer
months produce a sur-
prising crop of
hypothermia victims,
especially in higher
altitudes where sudden
rain and rapidly falling
temperatures are
common.

So, if someone in
your party becomes
hypothermic, seek help
(as always) and undress
him. Your ability to
effectively warm him is
extremely limited if you
hop into a sleeping bag
with him when he is soaking wet. Even if it is freezing outside and
you have to expose him to the elements for a few minutes—do it.
Dry him off and get dry clothes on him, then crowd as many warm
bodies as you have next to him, using all the sleeping bags you can
find. Administer hot drinks (only if he is conscious) until he begs you
to stop. If anyone has a rectal thermometer (very useful), use it peri-
odically to make sure his core temperature is rising.

In the unfortunate circumstance in which the victim is
extremely hypothermic and help is many hours away, you can try
what is referred to as a warm internal lavage. This is a polite way of
saying "stick a tube up his butt and fill him with warm water." Again,
this is reserved for imminently life-threatening hypothermia, as there
is some (small) medical risk, as well as a (fairly great) risk to the
friendship if you try this on a fully awake buddy who just caught a
chill. Again, the water bladder is the star here. Lubricate the tip and
gently insert it 4 to 5 inches (8 to 12 centimeters) into the rectum;
then gently squeeze in warm (not hot!) water. Most of the water will
run out, so think ahead and try to keep the person dry. This process
can turn into a huge mess, even in a sophisticated trauma room, but
continue, along with the other measures mentioned above.

Warm up with a warm-water enema!

HYPERTHERMIA

Hyperthermia represents the failure of the body's thermal-regulatory system at the other end of the spectrum. Unfortunately, there are not as many options when one is caught unprepared in an extremely hot environment. We can always put more clothes on, but there is a limit to how much we can take off. Equally unfortunate is that our bodies are much less forgiving of becoming too hot than too cold. Here is how we generally respond as our core temperature climbs:

DEGREES FAHRENHEIT	HOW YOUR BODY RESPONDS
98.6–100	• Sweating moderately to profusely
	• Having a feeling of being very hot
	• Panting
	• Moderate to severe thirst
100–103	• Profuse sweating, tapering off with rising core temperature
	• Feeling hot, starting to become less lucid
	• Extreme thirst when awake
103–106	• No sweating
	• Delirious to comatose
	• Seizures common at higher temperatures
	• Skin may become cool
> 106	• Coma and death, often within 1–2 hours

Unlike hypothermic victims, most severely hyperthermic individuals never recover once cardiopulmonary function stops. It is reasonable to attempt CPR while cooling is in progress, but it is typically fruitless. Therefore, it is imperative to prevent hyperthermia, if possible, and to treat it aggressively in the early stages if it does happen.

Our bodies have mechanisms to counteract the effects of a too-hot environment. For one, the skin's blood vessels open to act as a heat exchanger (a process called vasodilation). Also, we sweat. In a very hot environment—say, above 105°F (unless there is some wind that significantly aids in cooling), sweating represents the only real defense against the heat. Attempting to cool down a hot body by transferring excess body temperature to the outside air at Joshua Tree in July (120°F) goes against the laws of physics (these are the only laws I haven't figured out how to break). So, we sweat.

PREVENTION TIP

Move to Saskatchewan. In the unlikely event of a warm spell, fill your underwear with ice cubes; repeat.

MORE USEFUL PREVENTION TIP

When sweat reaches our skin, it immediately evaporates, cooling us. This is referred to by frizzy-headed geniuses as the "latent heat of evaporation." The less moisture in the air, the quicker sweat will evaporate. What this means is that for the same hot outside temperature, cooling will be more efficient in Yuma, Arizona (humidity 5%),

than Biloxi, Mississippi (humidity 98%). In very hot environments you may need to drink up to three liters per hour during exertion. As with everything, there are limits (except for the number of bean chalupas I can eat). Everyone's physiology is different, but at some point the heat will overwhelm us no matter how much we drink. It becomes critically important to replenish ourselves with more than water—the volume of electrolytes you lose through sweat in a very hot climate can be massive.

Fortunately, hyperthermia while paddling is fairly unusual, but it does happen, especially when you overdress for an early morning start. Then the sun comes out and you figure, "It's too much of a pain in the ass to take off the spray skirt, remove drysuit, etc." And what happens if you don't fill up your vascular cooling tank as fast as you sweat it out? Bingo!—rapid dehydration (page 20), followed quickly by hyperthermia.

TREATMENT

The cornerstone of treatment for a hyperthermic victim is fairly obvious: shade and drink. If available, give her cool fluids. That the coffee is fresh doesn't make it a great choice. Also, if there is enough water available, hose her down: I mean, soak the crap out of her. She can smack you later... after she thanks you for saving her life. Remember the latent-heat-of-evaporation thing mentioned above? Well, this is a perfect example. Take the victim's temperature rectally, if you have a rectal thermometer, and keep hosing her down until her temperature normalizes or she takes the hose (or thermometer) and sticks it in your ear.

In a very extreme situation, where fast cooling can be the difference between life and death, try the hose-up-the-butt trick again ("cold internal lavage," for you terminology sticklers). This time use only cold water (it doesn't do any good otherwise), and please don't make me beg you to be careful (I will if I have to, though). A liter of 110°F water from your CamelBak won't help lower a 105°F core body temperature.

...[5]...

FRACTURES AND DISLOCATIONS

Unfortunately, broken bones (fractures) are a common phenomenon among those gallivanting in the outdoors (please gallivant only where legal). Almost everything outside is harder and much more resistant to breaking than your bones (trees, rocks, and earth, for instance).

PREVENTION TIP
Wear a Kevlar body condom at all times.

MORE USEFUL PREVENTION TIP
Not much else to say. Wait, I know—be careful, look both ways before you cross the street, eat your vegetables, don't run with scissors...
    There are two basic types of broken bones: compound, and simple.

COMPOUND FRACTURES

With a compound fracture the bone either protrudes through the skin (gross!), or the skin is damaged over the area of a broken bone, regardless of whether you can see the bone. This doesn't apply to minor cuts or abrasions over a fracture. The only real difference between initially treating compound and simple fractures is that compound fractures can become infected much more readily.

Simple leg fracture

PREVENTION TIP

Talk to your bones before each outing. Impress upon them the importance of not breaking.

MORE USEFUL PREVENTION TIP

Since compound fractures are, one hopes, the result of an accident and not planned, be aware of the potential for falling (or being fallen on) and take all precautions to prevent falls.

TREATMENT

See the text on treatment below.

SIMPLE FRACTURES

I'll bet you've figured this one out. Yep, fracture with no exposed bone and no large laceration over the fracture site.

PREVENTION TIP

Again, have a chat with your bones on the importance of remaining intact. Emphasize teamwork.

Compound leg fracture

MORE USEFUL PREVENTION TIP

Same as for compound fractures. It's true that "the ground catches everything." No need to seek empirical evidence.

TREATMENT

So, what the heck do you do for your buddy when he breaks his leg? First, take a couple of deep breaths and try not to toss your trail mix, because the sight of a limb bending at unnatural angles, or the sound of snapped bones grating on each other can be really nauseating. As always, think "A-B-C" (page 24), then get the victim (or yourself, if alone) to a safe, warm, dry place, and arrange the injured area so that the pain is the least. Immediately after a bone is broken, the body initiates a defense response that results in massive swelling around the area. This represents eons of evolution—an attempt at an auto-splint, if you will. If the break is not otherwise apparent, this may be the main clue that a fracture exists. Next, you will need to look at both the injured area as well as the limb (assuming an extremity fracture) down toward the fingers or toes. This is because sometimes a broken bone may become displaced. No, not misplaced: displaced means that the bone's fragments are no longer in a normal, straight alignment. This may cause the fragment to kink, block, or even cut blood vessels inside the limb.

Why is this important, you ask? I'm glad you asked. It's important because a broken bone does not normally represent a life- or even limb-threatening emergency. You may even have days to get the injured person to definitive medical help without any

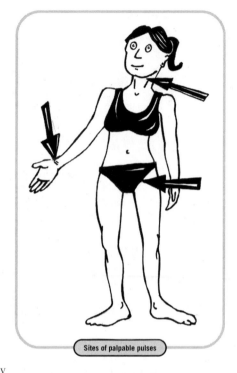

Sites of palpable pulses

negative consequences. If, however, the blood vessels (arteries, here) are blocked, the person may lose the extremity after only a single hour of ischemia (no blood flow). For instance, if your companion breaks her leg and you are not able to locate a foot pulse, you have to start thinking about impaired blood flow. To compare, feel for the pulse on the other foot (or hand, if it is the arm that is broken). If you can't feel the pulse here either, then it's probably one of three things: (1) you are feeling in the wrong area—recheck the diagrams and/or ask someone else to cop a feel; (2) the person is in shock, in which case the peripheral arteries (i.e., those at the wrist and ankle) will be clamped and hard to feel; or (3) the person is cold, in which case, again, the arteries will be clamped.

If the pulse on the injured side is absent or diminished, or if the hand or foot is cold or blue in comparison to the healthy one, you need to distract, or pull apart, the broken ends and then splint the extremity in such a way that the artery will not become recompressed

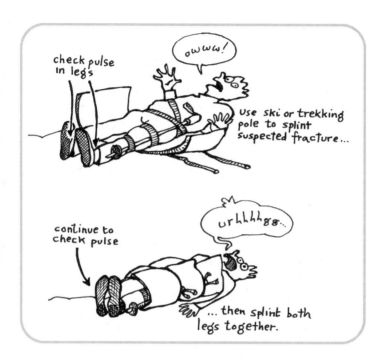

during transport to a hospital. You will not strengthen the bonds of a beautiful, loving relationship with your injured comrade when you do this, however. This process hurts like hell and should be done as quickly and efficiently as possible. If anyone has muscle relaxants (Valium, Flexeril, etc.) or painkillers (Demerol, ibuprofen, etc.), now would be a good time to administer them. Give the drugs 20 minutes or so to kick in and, as always, use them only as directed, do not mix medications, and make sure the victim is not allergic to the medication. Then make sure you have your splint materials ready to go.

Practice putting the splint on yourself so that you are not fumbling around trying to figure it out while your poor buddy is screaming in pain. Think about what you have at your disposal for a splint. Wrapping a sleeping pad (Ensolite or an inflatable) very tightly around the extremity while someone holds the extremity in distraction works very well. In other words, pull on the injured person's hand or foot until the pulse returns, then place straight sticks, spare paddles, or hiking poles on either side of the sleeping pad, and wrap the whole thing in duct tape. Do not wrap the duct tape (or straps, or whatever) too tightly! You don't want to place a great splint only to constrict the vessels with your wrap. Check the pulses in the affected foot or hand after you place the splint.

If splinting items are not available, then substitute what you have, but be sure you pad the extremity well. Keep in mind that you must immobilize the extremity one joint above and one below the fracture site. Otherwise the broken bones will move against each other. For example, with a broken lower leg, you must immobilize the knee and the ankle. This will result in a straight leg: the victim will have to use a buddy as a crutch to take all the weight off the injured leg, or be littered out.

If the bone is protruding or there is a large laceration over the fracture, place a clean gauze or handkerchief on the site and tape it in place before you place the splint. Do not dig around in the wound or worry too much about cleaning it. The emphasis here is splint, then transport the victim or await rescue.

There are several hundred bones in the body, so clearly we cannot cover the exact splinting mechanisms for all of them, but the concepts remain the same. Here are some special circumstances:

Facial Fracture
This usually looks awful, with lots of bleeding.

TREATMENT
There's not much to do here but stop the bleeding (apply pressure until it stops), and place a clean bandage over any lacerations.

Neck or Back Fracture
It will be unusual to *see* a fracture here, and you won't hear bones grate on each other. If conscious, the person will likely complain of severe pain at the fracture site. Unfortunately, the person may also be paralyzed below the level of the fracture (i.e., unable to move or feel any sensation).

TREATMENT
If she is unconscious, always treat her as if she has sustained a neck or back fracture. In other words, do not move her unless there is no choice. If you absolutely have to move her, you must have several

people available to log roll her onto a rigid stretcher. This means you have to keep the spine aligned all the way from the head to the legs. Someone will have to keep her head, neck, and shoulders moving as one unit. The reason this is so important is that, although she might have a broken back or neck, her spinal cord might be intact. If the victim is moved improperly, the bone fragments can shear the spinal column, resulting in permanent paralysis or even death (bet that got your attention!). She then has to be transported while strapped to the stretcher so that the spine doesn't move.

If she is conscious, you might be able to (gently) feel the area to see if it feels "boggy." This is another clue that a fracture exists. Even if it is obvious that the person has suffered paralysis, please be meticulous in handling the victim because the paralysis may be incomplete or even reversible.

Collarbone (Clavicle) Fracture
Usually, this injury occurs when you either receive a direct blow to the clavicle (paddle ricocheting off a boulder and slamming into it), or when you pitch forward downhill while portaging your kayak after having consumed too much Thunderbird the night before (actually *any* Thunderbird is too much). The fracture will be patently obvious because of the huge (lemon-sized) swelling where your straight-as-an-arrow collarbone used to be. Couple this with severe pain and an inability to pick your nose, and bingo! You have a diagnosis.

TREATMENT
Do not try to set or splint this; it will not work, and it will cause your buddy to suffer an embarrassing bout of incontinence from the pain. Simply place the arm against the body with the elbow bent at 90 degrees and wrap the arm and body together so that the arm cannot move. Again, do not wrap too tightly.

Rib Fracture
Do not do what John Wayne does (except when he rides his horse with the reins in his teeth—I love that!). In other words, don't wrap the chest with anything. All that does is constrict the victim's breathing and cause extreme pain. The fracture site(s) is (are) usually obvious because there is severe pain at the trauma site. You can feel the bones scrape each other if you compress the area ($10 word: crepitus). When

you push on the area, you will feel an immediate crushing blow to your cheek as your buddy slaps the crap out of you.

TREATMENT
Rib fractures really do hurt, and they cause the person to take rapid, shallow breaths. The most important thing to do is administer pain medicine and GOOD (get out of Dodge).

Finger and Toe Fractures

In light of other fractures such as a neck break or compound man-gling of your femur, just pretend that this will never happen. If it does, just laugh it off.

TREATMENT

Straighten it out as best you can and tape it to its neighbor (not too tight!—remember the swelling).

DISLOCATIONS

I would rather see a fracture than a dislocation in the ER any day; dislocations still make me go, "Ugghhhh!" (I try not to do that out loud.) Basically, dislocations occur when two bones that are normally kept in alignment with one another via ligaments and tendons pop out of those restraints and stick out at weird and disgusting angles. Unless one of the bones happens to break while becoming dislocated (a fairly common occurrence), the dislocated bone does not poke through the skin—thank God! Similar to fractures, dislocations do not typically represent life-threatening problems, but they do hurt like hell, and they begin to swell almost immediately—just like that girl Violet in *Willie Wonka and the Chocolate Factory* who chewed the experimental gum, swelled up into a giant blueberry, and had to be dejuiced by the Oompah Loompahs.

PREVENTION TIP

While falling, think, "Alignment, alignment, alignment... "

MORE USEFUL PREVENTION TIP

Just think ahead about how grossed out everyone is going to be.

TREATMENT

A significant amount of common sense and judgment go into field treatment of dislocations. As a general rule, it is best to immobilize the dislocated part with a sling or wrap and get to the ER quickly. Having said that, several other issues come into play here.

First, dislocations hurt like hell while the dislocation persists. It really may be more than the victim can bear if it will take more than several hours to reach definitive care.

Second, the dislocated bone may impinge on a nerve or artery, which in turn may result in the permanent functional loss of an extremity if the dislocation is not put back into place (reduced). Therefore, it may be necessary to try to reduce a dislocation in the field. *Warning:* This is a somewhat controversial and potentially dangerous (to the victim) remedy. This again represents both what I would anticipate myself doing and what I would imagine possible for nonmedical personnel to do. If at any time you, or the victim, feel as if the reduction process is not going well, stop, reassess, and probably cease your attempts. The danger is that the attempt to relocate the displaced bone may damage uninjured tissue—particularly by breaking the adjoining bone. To assess whether a nerve or artery (more important) is being compromised, feel for pulses beyond the dislocation site. Look to see if the injured arm or leg is paler than the other arm or leg, and gently pinch or lightly prick the skin of both arms (or legs) with a needle to see if sensation has been reduced in the damaged limb.

If either of the two above conditions exists, here is how to try to address several common dislocations.

Shoulder

Shoulder dislocations are probably the most common serious injury for paddlers. This is especially true for whitewater kayakers. This injury can occur at any time, but it most commonly occurs when one makes quick, aggressive paddle strokes in difficult rapids, or one plants the paddle to catch an eddy in fast water. Not surprisingly, these injuries occur proportionally more frequently in men (actually, that last statement holds true for essentially all athletic injuries—big muscles, vacuous skulls). Women typically learn excellent technique, or they don't do it at all. Men, on the other hand, will plop their hairy asses in the cockpit and muscle their way down the river after seeing kayaking for the first time on the Discovery channel—shoulder joints be damned. A stereotype, certainly, but also surprisingly valid.

Unfortunately, the shoulder is an extremely unstable joint and dislocates rather easily, particularly when one falls forward and arrests one's fall with an outstretched hand. Most shoulder dislocations are anterior (i.e., frontal). This means that the humerus (upper arm bone) pops forward out of the socket. For some people, this condition is chronic, and they know exactly how to reduce it themselves. By all means, let them do it themselves if possible. Just make sure

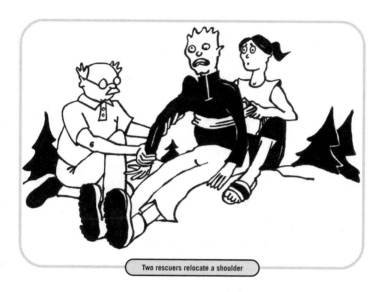

Two rescuers relocate a shoulder

you get far enough away so you don't toss your cookies when you hear that gross pop.

TREATMENT

Shoulder dislocations are amenable to field relocation and, in general, should be attempted as soon as possible after the dislocation. There are several reasons to relocate the shoulder quickly: first, it hurts like #$%@!, and your buddy will be forever in your debt for making him feel better. Second, as with all large-joint dislocations, there is a fair chance that the dislocated bone will impinge on a nerve or artery, potentially causing some permanent functional damage. Third, the dislocated shoulder looks really gnarly, and it is hard to pick up chicks (or guys) when you look like Quasimodo.

If the person is not able to relocate his own shoulder, then go ahead and give him some pain meds—usually ibuprofen. If you have a muscle relaxant, you may give that as well. Take the usual medication precautions: make sure there are no drug allergies or interactions with any other medications the person may be taking, and only give the prescribed dose. While the medications are kicking in, prepare for the fun time as follows:

(1) Place a jacket or blanket or something similar around his torso, and have him lie on his back.

(2) Have one rescuer hold the cloth tightly. This will keep the victim still while you are pulling on his arm. If a second rescuer is not available, you can use a rope in the same way, tying it to a tree, rock, or large moose.

(3) Next, take the victim's upper arm and pull directly away from his body. This will be somewhere around a 45-degree angle from his torso and in the same horizontal plane as the torso.

(4) While you are holding the arm as described in step 3 take the forearm and firmly (but slowly and sensitively!) rotate it outward (externally).

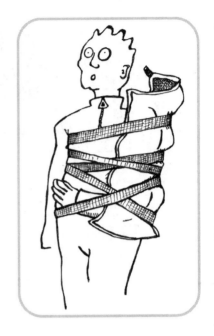

The victim now possesses the same upper extremity position as Princess Barbie when she addresses commoners. The force required will typically depend on how muscular the person is.

(5) Start very gently and consistently to increase the force. The shoulder relocates as the humerus starts to slide ever so slightly back into position, after which there is a rapid acceleration back into place. As the rescuer, you will feel the movement of the humerus under your fingers—it's rather sickening. This will then cause your anus to pucker audibly.

It is really important to have the person relax as much as possible (yeah, right!) so that the now-spastic muscles that are holding the bones in a dislocated position can be stretched enough to allow relocation.

In the fortunate event that the shoulder relocates, immediately place several hands on it to stabilize it (the shoulder may easily dislocate now, even with minor movements), and carefully but snugly strap the arm in a 90-degree position to the body. Now, get down to the ER.

Another way to do this (and the way we used to do it in the ER during residency) is to strap several empty water containers to the wrist

with duct tape (see, aren't you glad you brought that stuff?)—I have never used them, but I suspect that empty three-liter hydration bladders would work well. Then slowly fill the bladders with water. This is much easier on the puller, the pressure can be applied much more slowly and consistently, and the weights can be left hanging for a little while, during which the shoulder muscles have more time to relax.

Elbow

Don't mess with this one; the potential damage during relocation is too great.

TREATMENT

Just position the arm most comfortably for the victim (usually at a 90–degree bend), strap it against the body with an Ensolite pad and duct tape, and get help as quickly as possible.

Hip

Don't fool with this one either; there is almost always an associated fracture (acetabular, or "cup," fracture, for you minutiae freaks). The dislocation typically occurs posteriorly (to the back). The person will complain of severe hip pain—if conscious—and the upper leg (femur) will seem shorter even though you can't feel a fracture.

TREATMENT

A professional rescue is definitely in order here.

Fingers and Toes

OK, we can finally do something here with some (but not much) potential for damaging other tissues. Busted fingers and toes are pretty obvious—serious pain and swelling, and the digit looks like an outline of Florida.

TREATMENT

Here's the sequence:

(1) Give some ibuprofen or other mild pain medications to the victim (muscle relaxants are not necessary).

(2) Remove any minor children from the area; the imminent stream of compound expletives will cause deep and permanent psychic scars.

(3) Quickly, but not jerkily, pull outward and apply pressure from the appropriate side (the side where the bone is out of place). If the digit relocates, tape it to its buddy (loosely) and head to the ER so they can X-ray it to make sure there are no fractures.

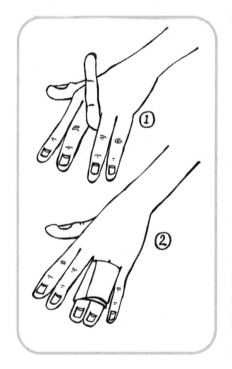

If it doesn't relocate fairly easily, or the pain is too much, immobilize it as best you can against its neighbor, and head on down the river.

...[6]...

OPEN WOUNDS
AND
LACERATIONS

The skin is a wonderful organ—it serves to keeps the ooky, gushy insides in and the dirty nasty environment out. When the skin's integrity is breached and the ooky gushy mixes with the dirty nasty, that's when the trouble starts. (Man, will my anatomy professor be pissed if she reads this.) That's the basics; if you do get a cut (laceration), scrape (abrasion), or other break in the skin, it is vitally important to minimize the amount of stuff that gets out (blood, muscles, tendons, etc.), as well as the stuff that gets in (dirt, twigs, Oreos, etc.).

PREVENTION TIP
Never, ever confuse an open Swiss Army knife with a roll of toilet paper in the middle of the night.

MORE USEFUL PREVENTION TIP
Really, not much else to say—just be careful around sharp stuff; a nasty laceration can end an excursion.

TREATMENT
How you treat a laceration will clearly depend on the type and location of the cut. A scrape on the leg, for instance, need not be as delicately handled as a cut on the inside of the nose. Here is the basic sequence:

(1) Stop the bleeding,

(2) Clean the area,

(3) Place an occlusive bandage over the area, and

(4) Seek medical help.

(STOP THE BLEEDING)

Really important, this blood thing. You only have about five quarts of the stuff running around in your body, so you may want to keep as much as you can. One of my very favorite teachers imparted to me an important fact concerning bleeding in the trauma situation: "There isn't any blood vessel outside the chest and abdominal cavities bigger than your finger." So, if you encounter bleeding, even scary, pulsating, massive bleeding—put your finger on it! Really, it will stop. If it doesn't stop completely, put two or three or four fingers on it, and push really, really hard. You will have to have something to brace yourself against—wrap your other fingers around the arm, place the injured leg against a log, and so on.

Many medical books recommend locating a pressure point in the armpit, groin, or elsewhere to compress to stop the bleeding. This doesn't work. I've tried it many times for gunshot wounds and for knife wounds to essentially all the major extremity arteries and veins just to see, but if you need to see for yourself, go ahead. If you do have a laceration of a major blood vessel, it may stop bleeding while you are holding pressure, only to start up immediately when you release. In this case you will just have to continue to hold pressure until you reach definitive medical help. Many times, however, bleeding will stop if you hold enough pressure to completely occlude the break in the blood vessel and allow the body's natural clotting mechanism to form a plug. This natural clotting may take 10 to 15 minutes or even longer. Keep checking every five minutes or so. If the bleeding is slowing down, keep the pressure on until it stops. If it does stop and it has been a very active bleeding site, don't bother cleaning it or looking for other injuries in the area, just cover it with a clean gauze or rag or whatever and get out of Dodge.

Another word here: despite what the well-intentioned emergency manuals recommend, do not place a tourniquet above a bleed-

ing site. It almost never works, and there is huge potential for causing additional harm. I have twice seen tourniquets that have been placed in the field. Both patients were still bleeding, and both had irreversible damage to tissue farther down the extremity that required additional disfiguring surgery to correct.

CLEAN THE AREA

Not much mystery here: makes sense to remove ($10 word: debride) the pine bark, marmot scat, and such from the open wound to reduce the infection risk. Only water, or water and mild soap, please. I know John Wayne used whiskey, but alcohol, peroxide, and other chemicals have the potential to damage tissue (nerves and blood vessels, primarily). Again, if there has been excessive bleeding, don't clean—or if you do—be gentle so you don't cause further bleeding.

PLACE AN OCCLUSIVE BANDAGE OVER THE AREA

Despite the advertised healing properties of bandages, they function exclusively to keep dirt out and do nothing to speed healing. Make sure you do not wrap bandages or anything else tightly around an extremity. This includes tape, Ace wraps, cords, and so on. Tight wraps completely encircling an extremity can make a no-big-deal situation into a devastating one by occluding either the venous or arterial blood flow.

SEEK MEDICAL HELP

Pull the bag of common sense out of your pack and apply it liberally here. You would obviously be unlikely to escape a week in the Canadian Rockies without some kind of battle wound, and you aren't going to run to the Mayo Clinic the first time you get a paper cut while opening a package of dehydrated Thai chicken, but do bear in mind that wounds are much more likely to become infected in the backcountry than in your living room. If the wound is large or deep or looks as though it may require stitches, alter your plans and zip into the nearest ER to have it checked out.

...[7]...

BACKCOUNTRY EVACUATION

Evacuation, for our purposes, will include getting the injured member of your party (perhaps yourself) to definitive medical care by one of two means: self-evacuation, or assisted evacuation.

SELF-EVACUATION

This is by far the most common, timely, and efficient method of getting yourself to help. Most situations that require us to abandon our plans and seek medical help are amenable to this type of rescue.

Obviously, not every situation can be covered in print. But when something does occur to you or a member of your party, sit and think for a minute. Major problems are a no-brainer. Snake bites, broken bones, and so on—you know to get help as quickly as possible. On the flip side, minor cuts, bruises, mild dehydration, or such, can be handled in the field, and you can usually continue on your way.

It is the tweener situation in which good judgment is demanded. These situations are legion: larger cuts, severe dehydration, diarrhea, hypothermia, and bad sprains. Even after 15 years of emergency experience, I've found that one of the most important tools I use is that little voice that pipes up immediately when an emergency occurs. You know the one I'm talking about. Call it your gut feeling, survival instinct, or whatever, but please listen to it. This advice applies even when you are in your first mile of a glorious two-week early-summer kayaking excursion down the Snake River with your new girlfriend (a Victoria's Secret underwear model who says that paddling Class-III water "just makes me horny") and you severely sprain your wrist while rodeoing in a stopper the size of a Volkswagen Jetta. Do you turn around and go to the ER, or tape the living crap out of your wrist? If you stop and think for a minute, the decision is almost always clear. Don't let your pride override your common sense.

OK, something has happened and you have to retreat. The questions to ask (go ahead and ask aloud):

(1) Can I get the injured person out without causing more damage?

(2) Can I get her out myself faster than if I called in outside assistance?

If the answer to both questions is yes, then make preparations and move out. If the answer to either question is no, then make preparations to seek outside help.

We will cover specific self-rescue situations in a minute, but first some comments on seeking outside help. The basic scenarios are listed below. I am assuming here that if anyone in your party has a working cell phone, satellite phone, or two-way radio, you will go ahead and use it to summon help.

Solo Traveler

Assume there is no method of outside communication (cell phone that actually has reception, satellite phone, or two-way radio with someone manning the other phone in civilization). Shame on you! There, I said it, but we'll get out the wet noodle later. Obviously, being incommunicado can present some very difficult decisions. In general, you are better off staying put, making your interim living situation as good as possible, and waiting for the cavalry. Clearly there are exceptions. For instance, no one knows where you are and when you might return, or you are in a situation where your injury or illness may significantly progress before you can reasonably expect help to come. In some of these situations you might be better off at least trying to move to a more conspicuous location.

Two Folks

Remember to ask the following three questions before mobilizing the injured person. The crux question here is almost always, "Should the uninjured person stay with the injured one or go off to seek help?" You will find hard and fast rules in most emergency medical books, but as anyone who has been in such a situation knows, there are multiple, subtle issues that go into deciding how to address this situation. Take a few minutes to objectively think out loud and open the extra-large box of common sense. Consider some things that are obvious and some that are not so obvious:

WHAT IS THE CONDITION OF THE UNINJURED PERSON?
Are they wiped from a 24-hour paddle down the Zambezi? How far is it to where you *know* there is help? What are the navigation skills of the injured person? Possible questions run ad infinitum. Focus, though, and really anticipate those that are pertinent to your situation. It is always possible to make a bad situation hopeless by rushing a decision right after a medical emergency.

HOW FAR AWAY IS HELP?
Maybe it would be more expeditious to have someone with a fractured ankle use you as a crutch for a half mile than to radio for help and have to wait until morning for the chopper. But this would probably not be a reasonable decision in the hinterlands along the Salmon River 12 miles from the nearest jeep road.

WHAT IS THE CONDITION OF THE INJURED PERSON?
Strangely, the more severely injured or ill the person is, the more likely it is that you will have to leave him to seek help. This is counterintuitive to most of us ("I'm not leaving you, dude!"), however, there is likely not much you can do in the field except delay the retrieval of professional help.

Three or More Travelers
The best of a bad situation: common sense would dictate that one person (or more) stay with the victim and one (or more) go get help. Go common sense! This is exactly what to do. Do take a minute to sort out who goes where. It probably doesn't make much sense to send an overweight, elderly, out-of-shape trauma surgeon 15 miles over hill and dale for help, leaving the 19-year-old NCAA cross-country champion to patch up someone who has just flown his playboat 60 feet into a shallow pool.

(SEEKING OUTSIDE HELP)

As the title suggests, this entails summoning help—usually professional—from outside your immediate party. Clearly, if the situ-

Leave an itinerary and return time with someone who loves you.

ation is so dire that you can't go or send a member of your party, then you should call the closest professional organization: 911, sheriff's office, ranger station, rescue center, or such. In this case it would be extremely helpful to have spoken with a ranger or similar personnel before setting out so that if an emergency did arise, they would at least have some passing notion of who and where you were. (I know. You're an experienced paddler. You don't need a babysitter, etc.) Even if you have only an emergency phone number, call without having spoken to the ranger or sheriff beforehand: it still may save some time and aggravation.

I have heard many horror stories of people calling 911 for an emergency and spending 30 precious cell-phone minutes trying to explain to an operator that there is no street address. Still, call 911 if you don't have a better choice.

How to execute a professional evacuation is beyond the scope of this book. I will say only that when the pros do arrive, please stay out of the way and do exactly what they say. This especially applies to medical personnel. I can't tell you how many times I have witnessed medical personnel at a scene trying to take over or bully rescue personnel. The trained rescue personnel have done these rescues hundreds of times in horrid outdoor conditions. The only thing you can accomplish by trying to impose your will or ego on the situation is to delay care for the victim. *Remember:* you summoned them for their assistance; let them assist. In these circumstances I will identify myself and ask if they would like any assistance. If they say yes, I ask what they would like me to do. If they say no, I get out of the way.

...[8]...

ANIMAL AND INSECT BITES

OK, you're in the great outdoors; what are the odds that you will see wild critters? Probably pretty high. What are the odds that you will be bitten or stung by one? Again, likely greater than while sitting at Starbuck's, slurping a double vanilla latte. It just depends on how curious you are. To be prepared, though, go ahead and plan on exchanging protein with a wild beast—then you won't have to waste valuable time shrieking, thrashing, and amusing the 10-year-old boys of Troop 56 who happen to be passing by as you flail at the scorpion stinger embedded in your tush. We talk about this issue before heading into the backcountry because this is one of the areas where bad things can still happen despite exhaustive preparations.

Ouchy animal and insect encounters, of course, be greatly reduced with simple planning. But this text will in no way attempt to deliver a treatise on distinguishing between a pug-nosed rattler and a pygmy rattler, or even describing how a neurotoxin from one species varies in effect from the endotoxin of another. In the field the sub-genus of poisonous insect or reptile that bit you really makes no difference. I'm sure I would be too freaked out (oops, that violates the no-panic rule) to give a crap about species identification if I had a rattler hanging off my leg. Having said that, it is vitally important that you do *try* to identify whether or not the critter that bit or stung you is poisonous. Was it a rattlesnake or a nonpoisonous bull snake? Is the welt on your elbow from a scorpion or a fire ant? If it is a poisonous beast such as a rattlesnake or scorpion and you can safely capture the thing (alive or dead), take it with you to the ER. This will help personnel there determine which antitoxin to administer, if any. Before you head outdoors, it really is worth taking the time to look at a good book with color pictures, such as one from Menasha Ridge Press's *Dangerous Wildlife* series, that identifies the potentially dangerous critters in your proposed travel area.

There are three broad categories of bites and stings: those of bugs, those of reptiles, and those of mammals.

BUGS

Bites from the members of this category are probably the least preventable of the three. Unlike for mammals and reptiles, you may actually represent a food source for insects. I also think that their brains aren't big enough for them to know to avoid you; they're also ugly, and creepy, and...

Wasps, Bees, and Hornets

Wasp, bee, and hornet stings don't present an emergency except in the following two scenarios:

Scenario 1—Someone in the party has a known hypersensitivity to the venom of these critters. This type of allergy causes a severe asthma-like reaction in which the airways shut down. That person should always, and especially in the backcountry, carry a prepackaged vial of epinephrine (adrenaline), called an epi-pen.

PREVENTION TIP
Wasps, bees, and hornets hate clowns. So dress like a clown.

MORE USEFUL PREVENTION TIP
Don't aggravate anything with a stinger. Check outhouses before you rush in and knock down a wasp nest. Also be mindful of ground nests, which may be difficult to spot. Yellow jackets, especially, like to keep hearth and home in abandoned rodent burrows.

TREATMENT
Without an *immediate* injection of epinephrine, the victim will usually die, often in five to ten minutes. Please make sure that everyone

in the party knows this beforehand and actually examines the epi-pen in the living room the night before departure and discusses how to use it. It involves injecting the entire contents of the syringe under the skin, usually in the arm.

The epi-pen is part of my standard first-aid kit (see appendix) for a few reasons: Someone can have a hypersensitivity potential and not know it. Or he may know about it but have forgotten his epi-pen or may require more than one injection.

If he has been stung by one of the flying critters and starts to wheeze like he has asthma, *do not* wait. Give the injection, or have him give himself the injection immediately. I have seen people wait "to see if it gets any worse" at the start of a hypersensitivity reaction before giving a shot of epinephrine. Trust me, it will get worse—to the point of death.

Scenario 2—Someone without a hypersensitivity reaction has been stung multiple (usually more than ten) times. This may deliver enough venom, even to someone who is not particularly sensitive to it, to trigger a hypersensitivity-type reaction.

TREATMENT
Again, if the person begins to have trouble breathing, administer the epinephrine. It should go without saying that if someone has trouble breathing, whether epinephrine was administered or not, you must get him to the ER—yesterday. Even if he does not demonstrate signs of troubled breathing, if he has been stung multiple times, it is a good idea to at least get him back to civilization, if not to a hospital. There have been cases of delayed hypersensitivity reactions, particularly after multiple stings or bites.

Scorpions
You know what these critters look like—evil incarnate. A scorpion grabs its prey (or your toe) with its nonpoisonous front crablike claws and then injects a paralyzing venom from a stinger at the end of its whiplike tail. In other words, stay away from its butt. The poor victim is typically stung when she puts all or part of her body into a partially enclosed space into which a scorpion has crawled for a snuggly nap. This includes putting a foot into a hiking boot that has been left outside the tent at night, crawling into a sleeping bag that has been left unrolled with the tent flap open, and so on. I grew up in New Mexico where scorpions are raised on ranches for their meat (OK, if you don't believe that, how about jackalope farms?). OK, OK, but there are a lot of them, and fortunately, even though I have seen plenty, I have never been on the pointy end of one.

PREVENTION TIP
Call in an air strike the day before your climb to obliterate all living creatures within a five-mile radius of your proposed campsite.

MORE USEFUL PREVENTION TIP

Think like a scorpion; that is, keep your tent zipped up, your pack off the ground in a plastic garbage bag, your boots in your tent, and so on.

TREATMENT

Most scorpions—with the exception of some species in Arizona and Mexico—are not particularly hazardous to humans. The stings are painful but are not typically life-threatening. The sequence of treatment here is ice the site, elevate the stung body part above the level of the heart, use ibuprofen to reduce the swelling, and head to the nearest ER. If you can retrieve the critter, go ahead and take it with you.

Spiders

I know it's not in line with the teachings of Buddha, but I don't like 'em. Unfortunately (or maybe fortunately), you don't usually see the spider before, during, or after the bite.

PREVENTION TIP

Spiders love clowns. So do not dress like a clown.

MORE USEFUL PREVENTION TIP

Beware of outhouses. Spiders such as the black widow have been known to take up residence around the drop hole. Guys should especially be careful of dangling down a dark hole anything warm that might be of interest to a cold, curious spider.

Fortunately, almost all spiders are essentially harmless to humans (at least in the United States). A few common exceptions are:

BROWN RECLUSE

These small (2-centimeter), brown critters with a violin tattooed on their backs are relatively common in the United States. But people almost never see these guys. Bite victims typically report a moderately painful bite but don't seek treatment for days or weeks as the area around the bite begins to die ($10 term: tissue necrosis). In other words, there won't be any symptoms, or even anything to do, on a typical weeklong paddling trip.

TREATMENT

If you do happen to catch the critter that bit you, go ahead and collect the nasty little beast and get to the ER . . . ASAP. There is a drug that, when administered right after a brown recluse bite, can help minimize tissue damage.

BLACK WIDOW

Here's a creature worthy of nightmares. The female kills and eats the male after copulation—talk about performance anxiety! This dominatrix typically inhabits dark, cool places like basements, caves, hollowed logs, and so on. You will be much more likely to see and feel this gal if she bites you, compared to a brown recluse. The bite is much more painful and may start swelling right away.

TREATMENT

Again, take the thing with you if you can do so safely, and head to the hospital right away. Unlike the brown recluse's venom, the toxin of a black widow will spread throughout your system and make you very sick. The earlier you receive treatment, the less sick you will become. No field treatment is required here.

TARANTULAS

Eeeeeekkk! These are slow, relatively ponderous arachnids that are pretty easily avoided. Their bite is locally very painful but not particularly hazardous overall.

TREATMENT

Ice, elevation, ibuprofen. Head to the ER if the bite area starts to look red or purulent, that is, "full of pus."

REPTILES

You might encounter any of a variety of reptiles in the great outdoors, but snakes are the big kahuna, the grand pooh-bah: the biggest fear most people have when venturing into the backcountry. While it is certainly possible to meet with a snake, these critters are probably the easiest of all potentially dangerous beings to avoid. They are petrified (OK, they didn't actually say it, but they sure act scared) of humans. As a child, my buddy and I would live for summer, when our favorite activity was catching snakes (nonpoisonous, and, no, we didn't hurt them. They always tried to escape. The only time they would try to bite was when we had our grubby little hands on them.

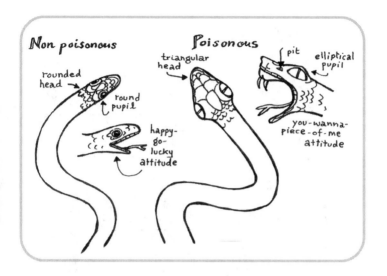

The same holds for poisonous snakes. They have absolutely no inter-est in wasting their time or venom biting you, because you are not prey. Therefore, if you make a little noise, travel at a reasonably slow pace, and stay somewhat vigilant, you will greatly reduce your chance of a snake encounter.

Although a musky rat snake may give you the willies, we are really interested here only in the bite of a poisonous snake. Once again, it would behoove you to consult a color text before you find yourself in a position in which you might actually encounter a snake. Most poisonous snakes have triangular heads (at least in the United States; all bets are off in distant lands). This wicked shape allows them space to sheathe those scary fangs. There are exceptions, how-ever. The red-, yellow-, and black-banded coral snake, for instance, has the typical bullet-shaped head of a nonpoisonous snake. For the coral snake, remember the adage, "Red next to black is a friend of Jack. Red next to yellow will kill a fellow."

PREVENTION TIP
Only venture into areas where reptiles are made to feel unwelcome. If you see a reptile, make fun of it and say something like, "We don't like your kind around here."

MORE USEFUL PREVENTION TIP

Put yourself in a snakeskin (no, not snakeskin boots! PETA will be all over me). Snakes are cold-blooded (not a very accurate term, but one with which we are all familiar). In other words, unlike mammals' bodies, which maintain a constant body temperature, a snake's body warms or cools according to the temperature of the environment. So, on hot days when it is cooler under rocks, overhangs, tree branches, and so on, guess what? Yep, Snakesville, USA. Similarly, when the sun goes down in the desert Southwest and the temperature plummets, guess who else may head for the deep recesses of that 800-fill down bag? Bulky Ranger Bob? Buxom Ranger Sue? Nope.

TREATMENT

If you are unfortunate enough to be bitten, try to ascertain the snake's color, whether there are rattles, the shape of head, and so on. Don't bother to try to collect the critter unless there is absolutely no risk of someone else's being bitten. The antivenom used to treat bites is the same regardless of species, and even dead snakes can envenomate (their nervous systems can stimulate the jaws to bite and the poison sacs to expel venom. Again, venomous snakes typically leave two puncture marks, not the parabolic jaw imprint of a nonpoisonous snake. In this scenario, you must get to the nearest ER, now! Patient outcome after snake envenomation depends almost entirely on how quickly the victim receives definitive care. Having said that, it is also imperative that the patient move as little as possible. Muscular action (such as walking) serves to pump the poison faster through the circulatory system. The tricky part is trying to both minimize movement and quickly effect an evacuation. Clearly, if a five-minute walk will save six hours of rescue time, then do it. If, on the other hand, the time it would take you to walk to help would be about the same as if your buddy ran to summon the Mounties, then stay put.

The only self-treatment you should think about is to clean the area and place a clean bandage on the wound, then elevate the body part and put ice or something else cold on the bite, if you have it. Never cut the area and try to suck out the poison. Besides being really gross, this will do absolutely no good and can potentially do serious damage. Also, never place a tourniquet on a bitten extremity unless you intensely dislike the person and wish to see them eventually lose a limb.

MAMMALS

Obviously, there are far too many animals in this category to mention every one; however, I'll hit the big concerns.

Rodents

Rodents typically bite humans only after they have been systematically domesticated by being fed in touristy areas, or when cornered—

such as when they find themselves in the bottom of your pack as you reach for another granola bar.

PREVENTION TIP
Let a rat bite you before you leave home. What are the odds that you will be bitten twice?

MORE USEFUL PREVENTION TIP
Don't feed the chipmunks, and keep your gear sealed up, right? Unfortunately, that just won't cut the mustard. Mice and other rodents are persistent and often ingenious in their assaults, and many species of mammals—not just bats—carry rabies. So take care to store food properly whenever you stop to camp.

TREATMENT
If you are bitten, try to take the critter with you to the ER (alive, if possible). You were going to go to the ER without my having to tell you, weren't you? Rodents will typically not inflict a very serious wound (except for that rabbit in Monty Python's *Search for the Holy Grail*), so just clean the wound with soap and water, and place a clean gauze over it.

Large Cats

Realistically, the mountain lion is the only critter in this category that poses even a remote threat. In some western states where humans have almost completely wiped out a cougar's territory, there have been isolated attacks. These have typically come from young male cats without a biped-free territory of their own, or older cats that have to hunt us slow humans instead of their natural fast, herbivore prey. The victims are almost always attacked from behind, and almost all attacks have resulted in death or severe mauling.

PREVENTION TIP
Keep a litter box between you and the lunging animal. The cat will want to use the litter box.

MORE USEFUL PREVENTION TIP
Check ahead about the likelihood of encountering a mountain lion in your travel area. Cats like to leap down on prey, so you might want to keep that in mind in areas where mountain lions are known to live.

TREATMENT

Treatment here is beyond the scope of this book and consists primarily of stopping serious bleeding with direct pressure, and summoning professional help as quickly as possible. One victim, attacked near Denver, managed to free his head from a cougar's mouth by reaching up and gouging out one of the cougar's eyes. I guess the lesson here is to fight like hell. It's probably the only chance you have.

Bears

Bear bites, as with all types of wild-animal bites, usually result from something that we humans did wrong, like feeding the bears, getting too close to a sow with cubs, and so on.

PREVENTION TIP

Carry a Smokey the Bear coloring book with you. Statistics prove that you are extremely unlikely to be attacked by a bear while coloring.

MORE USEFUL PREVENTION TIP

Avoid bear contact if possible. Store your food in bear-proof containers. Cook and store food well away from where you plan to hang out and sleep.

TREATMENT

Unfortunately, bear bites usually end up as severe mauling injuries and will be covered in the Miscellaneous chapter under "Massive Trauma" (page 79).

Humans

The most serious bites that do not involve large wounds are from the mouths of Homo sapiens. A bite here usually refers to an inadvertent cut on the hand or other body part through accidental contact with a buddy's tooth. The risk here is infection caused by the wide and repulsive repertoire of bacteria that inhabits our mouths (yes, yours too).

PREVENTION TIP

Do not hang out with toddlers, vampires, or cannibals.

MORE USEFUL PREVENTION TIP

One hopes you will have the luxury of worrying about something else.

TREATMENT

Usual advice: clean with soap and water, apply a clean bandage, and go to the ER. I almost always give patients a course of antibiotics, so unless it's really just a tiny scratch, go see the doc. For an entertaining discussion regarding sexual encounters in relation to biting behavior, check out Buck Tilton's *Sex in the Outdoors*.

...[9]...

MISCELLANEOUS

MASSIVE TRAUMA

If possible, send for help *now*. Massive trauma represents an extremely difficult area even for extensively trained personnel. Seeing someone, especially someone close to you, who has taken a long fall or been mauled by a bear will obviously be incredibly upsetting. He will almost certainly have suffered multiple severe injuries.

PREVENTION TIP
Limit trauma to something short of massive—minimal trauma being preferable.

MORE USEFUL PREVENTION TIP
Not much to say here, except use your head. Definitely be prepared for the inevitable, but also keep in mind the possibility of the improbable.

TREATMENT
Really, the only recourse you have is to break a very complicated situation into a series of simple steps. As always, A-B-C first! In other words, if they ain't breathing, or they don't have a pulse, nothing else you do will matter. If you do an A-B-C check and all signs point to

respiratory and/or cardiac arrest, start CPR immediately (page 23). After successfully resuscitating him (or stopping after you have done your best (page 29), make sure that he (and others in the party) are not in imminent danger (lying in a flash flood zone, trapped in a grizzly's mouth, etc.), then look for problems that could cause his immediate demise, such as serious bleeding. Treat this by direct pressure as described in chapter 6. You will have to detach yourself somewhat from the ongoing drama and view the emergency as something like a model airplane to be put together using the instruction manual. You don't try to glue everything in one step; you take one step at a time. If you don't do this, dealing with someone who is a bloody mess from head to toe will overwhelm you.

Continue your survey of the victim, treat the most serious problem, then move to the next-most-serious issue in turn. To avoid worsening a covert spinal-cord injury, do not move him, if possible. Fractures (other than of the vertebrae or skull) are usually not of immediate concern and should be taken care of (page 43) after the life-threatening issues are dispensed with.

At some point the victim will certainly slip into shock. Even in hospitals you may hear that someone has gone into shock. Many medical personnel use the term loosely and do not understand what it means. Shock is an esoteric, poorly defined term, but for our purposes it means that sometime shortly (usually 1 to 15 minutes) after a major trauma, the victim becomes less responsive—even to the point of unconsciousness, blood pressure drops, and the skin pales. Shock is likely a survival response to shut down nonvital systems and may happen abruptly. Don't fret or lose focus if he goes into shock. Just continue the treatment discussed above.

After the serious bleeding has stopped (or someone is still holding pressure) and fractures are aligned, insulate him from the ground and keep him warm. Position him so his head is slightly higher than his heart (particularly if he has sustained a head injury; this will help lower the pressure in the head). Do everything you can to get help quickly.

In almost every situation in which someone has been very seriously injured it is unwise to try to move, or "litter," him to help.

Of course there may be situations in which no amount of on-scene medical attention will save a massively injured person. These might include major head or spinal-cord trauma, a collapsed lung (or

two), a ruptured spleen, or a ruptured major internal blood vessel (such as the aorta), among many other possibilities. I hope you will never have to face such a situation, but if you do, remember that all you can do is all you can do. (Buddha said that first, I think. Or was it Grandma?) A victim who is that critically injured would likely have died even if the surgeon general had been present.

LIGHTNING INJURIES

I grew up and live in the Southwest, where summer thunderstorms occur almost daily—and I think that lightning really is a thunderbolt from Zeus. But I digress; lightning obviously represents one of nature's most impressive and frightening spectacles. Unfortunately, lightning kills about a hundred people in the United States every year. Unlike many other dangers (such as a wolf attack), lightning is a real threat.

PREVENTION TIP
Only paddle indoors at the YMCA pool.

MORE USEFUL PREVENTION TIP

Since lightning does not strike out of a clear blue sky, try to become familiar with the weather patterns where you will be traveling, especially if you will be in an area that you have not previously visited. Most places have relatively predictable seasonal weather patterns, which may include thunderstorms. Ranger stations have a wealth of information on lightning and countless other topics. I think the rangers are particularly interested because they are the ones who will have to rescue your smoked butt if you are struck.

Remember that on large bodies of water or areas where trees or other high points are scarce, you will be the tallest object around. Think about it.

Also be aware that cloud-to-ground lightning strikes have been recorded over a distance of 20 miles!

If you do find yourself in a lightning storm, and you can safely scramble to shore, do so. Then stop and take all metal objects out of a pack or dry bag, squat on top of it with all your body parts off the ground, and wait for the storm to pass. Please note that if you have a pack with any metal in the (internal or external) frame, take out a sleeping pad and squat on that, away from your pack. Even if it is spewing raindrops the size of gopher heads, do not seek shelter under a tree, or a rocky overhang. Rocks conduct electricity.

TREATMENT

There are two basic types of injury patterns from lightning: those from direct hits, and those from ground conduction (indirect strikes).

DIRECT HITS

As you would expect, these are usually (but not always) immediately fatal. Clearly, the most pressing issue related to lightning strikes of either type is the massive electrical charge that rushes through the body, which damages the heart's electrical system. The heart may be jolted into an irregular rhythm ($10 term: cardiac dysrhythmia), which in turn leads to sudden cardiac arrest. If someone has been struck, immediately check breathing and pulse (remember A-B-C), and start CPR if appropriate. Surprisingly, a reasonably high percentage of people do survive direct hits, so be relatively persistent with CPR.

If your buddy survives a direct hit, run immediately to the nearest convenience store and buy a lottery ticket; no wait, that's not right—OK send someone for help. A strike victim can relapse into an

abnormal heart rhythm and subsequently suffer cardiac arrest, so have someone get rescue personnel—yesterday. Do not try to move the victim, unless she is in imminent danger.

A direct-hit lightning-strike victim will have an entry wound and an exit wound. In a typical scenario, a strike on top of the head exits the big toe. For you hunters, the effect is something like that of a hollow-point bullet: a very small entry site—possibly undetectable—and a huge blown-out exit area. Yuck! Unfortunately, lightning is a very strong electrical current that travels through the best conductors available—nerves and blood vessels, in this case. This current typically causes massive trauma to extremities or internal organs, which must be dealt with quickly by the nearest burn or trauma unit.

There is not really much else you can do at the scene except the common-sense stuff—keep the victim warm, dry, and insulated from the ground, with the head higher than the feet, and clean and bandage any wounds.

INDIRECT HITS

Much more survivable than direct hits, these are plenty lethal nonetheless. Again, lightning conducts via the best conductors, which, in order of conductivity are metal, water, rock, and earth. This means that one lightning strike has the potential for one (usually) direct hit but multiple indirect injuries.

The issues here are the same: cardiac arrest, electrical burns, and internal trauma. In the case of an indirect hit, however, you usually don't find entry and exit sites. Treat these hits the same as direct strikes.

DEHYDRATION

This term is thrown around frequently, and we all possess some vague idea of what it means, but sitting down and explaining it accurately can be difficult. A brief description of how the body functions is in order here. Wait, don't go screaming off into the night; it's pretty simple. Although much more complicated than the fluid system in your car, the fluid system in your body behaves much the same way (*warning:* do not change your blood every 3,000 miles!). If your fluid output from sweating, urinating, and breathing (this represents a large fluid loss, particularly when breathing hard at a high altitude in a dry climate) consistently exceeds your intake (drinking), your internal fluid volume will decrease and you will officially become dehydrated. You can get your official "I'm Dehydrated" patch at most outdoor shops. Your amazing body can compensate your loss of precious bodily fluid within limits, by pulling fluids from other fluid-filled spaces in your body (much too involved to get into here).

As with most things in life, there are varying degrees of badness with regard to dehydration. These range from feeling thirsty (not too bad) to having big chunks of icky proteins clogging the kidney's filtering mechanism, causing complete renal shutdown (pretty darn bad). Dialysis machines are not only expensive but also very heavy.

PREVENTION TIP

Drink some liquids.

MORE USEFUL PREVENTION TIP

Drink a whole lot of fluids. Really, this is one area where valid excuses should be rare. With the availability of water bladders (CamelBak, Platypus, etc.) that you can stick in your pack and suck on anytime, dehydration should become like smallpox: a threat no longer.

To continue, what you drink is equally important. When you sweat, you exude not only water but also what are called electrolytes—primarily sodium, potassium, and chloride. If you replenish only with water, you will dilute the diminished electrolytes in your bloodstream. Fortunately, your body has an amazing capacity to autocorrect this, but there are limits. There have been many examples of high-level athletes drinking an excessive amount of water for an extended period and suffering from a severe electrolyte imbalance called hyponatremia (not enough sodium); some have even died from this. This obviously represents an extreme situation, but you will help your body out a lot, as well as markedly improve your performance, if you replenish with an electroltye–carbohydrate drink such as Gatorade, Cytomax, or Gookinaid.

Clearly, everyone is different both in size and physiologic makeup, but as a guideline, somewhere around one liter per hour of fluid intake during heavy exertion (no, not that type of exertion) should be about right. If you pee relatively clear urine about every two to four hours, you know you are drinking enough fluids.

TREATMENT

For field purposes, the primary treatment for someone who is dehydrated is obviously to get him to drink. Severe dehydration can lead to stupor and unconsciousness. In this situation, do not try to force him to take liquids; he may choke, and then you will have someone who is not only severely dehydrated but not breathing either. The priority here is to fetch help fast. If no help is forthcoming, you can try something that seems pretty weird—flow fluids into a person's rectum, where the body will absorb them. You can't achieve a huge volume repletion, but it may be possible to replete their fluids enough so that they can take fluids by mouth. I have not personally tried this, nor do I know anyone who has, but rectal absorption is routinely used to administer medications for quick absorption. I would take the mouthpiece off a water-bladder tube, lubricate the tubing end, and gently insert it two to three inches (five to seven centimeters) into the rectum. Do not force it! It should pass easily. Place the victim on his side for this, if possible. Raise the water bladder above the patient and gently squeeze the bladder to force in some fluid (think Fleet's enema). Some fluid will likely leak out, but be relatively persistent. If the above-mentioned water bladder were mine, I would donate it to the person after he recovers.

DENTAL EMERGENCIES

For our purposes, dental emergencies usually consist of broken teeth, lost fillings, or lost or broken crowns. They are clearly not life threatening, but typically hurt. Anyone who has had a dental misfortune in the out-of-doors will definitely attest to the briskness of the sensation that occurs when one sucks air across a damaged tooth.

PREVENTION TIP
Eat sugary foods constantly, starting at age 8. Don't brush your teeth. Get full dentures at age 20 and only then start your paddling career.

MORE USEFUL PREVENTION TIP
Take care of the ivories! You don't get any more. See your dentist often, and especially before an international adventure. You may be surprised to learn that novocaine can be hard to find in many exotic locales.

TREATMENT
There are two general things to do here:

(1) Apply clove oil to the damaged dentition. This is very effective and is a long-lasting dental painkiller—a must-have for the medical kit, especially for protracted backcountry forays or foreign travel.

(2) If you are incredibly compulsive, or suspect that you may have some poor dental work (probably should have had that fixed before paddling the Northwest Passage, huh?), you can get a product from your dentist or pharmacist to use as a temporary filling. Several brands are available; Temparin, a paraffin-based filler, is a common one. It can potentially salvage a paddling expedition. You simply use the applicator to fill the exposed cavity. I have known people to try their own field fix with mashed-up paper, tubers, epoxy, and other substances. I have not heard of any of these working even for a short period, but I'm sure their efforts provided hours of high-quality entertainment for their companions.

APPENDIX:
MY MEDICAL KIT

Small, medium, and large Band-Aids

Blister bandages such as DuoDerm or other hydrocolloidal dressings

Sterile gauze pads

Duct tape wrapped around a Nalgene water bottle. You can do brain surgery with this stuff. Very easy to unwrap from a water bottle, as opposed to a skinny trekking pole.

Tampons (for nasal packing, you goofball!); nasal tampons, if you can find them

Purell or other waterless hand sanitizer

Ibuprofen (compound from the gods, magic pills, Rocky Mountain M&Ms)

Antidiarrheal medicine (Lomotil, Imodium)

Antireflux medicine (Maalox, Zantac, Prilosec, etc.)

Phenergan suppositories, 25 mg (prescription medication to be taken only with the consent of and by prescription from your doctor). This is an antinausea medication ($10 word: antiemetic); remove the foil wrapper and stick it in the pooper of someone who is puking his brains out.

Ciprofloxacin, 500 mg (antibiotic), 4 to 6 tablets; by prescription only—above restrictions apply

Epi-pen (epinephrine syringe for injection during life-threatening allergic reactions); you definitely must talk to your own doctor about obtaining and using this.

Clove oil—for toothaches, broken teeth

Temparin brand temporary filling for field-damaged dental work

Rectal thermometer

Repeat disclaimer—this is what I usually take. Some of these medications are by prescription only and may be taken only with the consent of your doctor after careful review of your medical history and drug allergies.

Obviously, you can add much more to your medical kit, but as always there is a weight/space/necessity trade-off: "What will I really need?" versus "Hey! I just ran the upper Gauley with a heart-bypass machine."

If you plan on traveling to a foreign country, definitely overstock on medical supplies—you can always leave some at a base location.

INDEX

…notes…

...notes...

…notes…

…notes…

...notes...

ABOUT THE
AUTHOR

Emergency medical expert PATRICK BRIGHTON is active in many outdoor activities including backpacking, mountain biking, ice/rock climbing, and kayaking. Dr. Brighton works part-time as a general surgeon and full-time building a house out of old tires. He and his wife Kimberley live in Montrose, Colorado.